# GEOPOLITICS
## OF GLOBALIZATION

## Networked Americas

## Romanovski Zephirin

ISBN 978-1-63814-120-4 (Paperback)
ISBN 978-1-63814-121-1 (Digital)



Covenant Books
11661 Hwy 707
Murrells Inlet, SC 29576
www.covenantbooks.com

# CONTENTS

# LIST OF TABLES

# LIST OF ABBREVIATIONS

| | |
|---|---|
| ALBA | The Bolivarian Alliance for the Peoples of Our America |
| ARUAG | Agence régionale d'urbanisme et d'aménagement de la Guyane |
| ASEAN | Association of Southeast Asian Nations |
| CACM | Central American Common Market |
| CAN | Andean Community |
| CARICOM | Caribbean Common Market |
| CCSCS | Coordinadora de Centrales Sindicales del Cono Sur |
| CCSPJP | Citizen Council for Public Security and Criminal Justice |
| CDH | Departmental Council of Habitat |
| CEPAL | Comision Economica Para Latin America (or in English ECLAC) |
| CGT | Centrale guyanaise des travailleurs (the main Guyanese Labor Union) |
| CINM | Council of the National Institute of Migration |
| CSR | Corporate Social Responsibility |
| DDE | Direction départementale de l'équipement |
| DESAL | Center for Economic and Social Development of Latin America |
| DIV | Direction inter-ministerielle à la ville |
| DSU | Développement social urbain (or in English, Urban Social Development) |
| DSQ | Développement social des quartiers (or Social Development of Neighborhoods) |

| | |
|---|---|
| DTO | Drug Trafficking Organizations |
| ECLAC | Economic Commission for Latin America and the Caribbean |
| EPAG | Etablissement public foncier et d'aménagement de la Guyane |
| ETUC | European Trade Union Confederation |
| EU | European Union |
| EZLN | Zapatista Army of National Liberation |
| FDG | Democratic Guyanese Forces (in English) |
| FOCEM | Mercosur Structural Convergence Fund |
| FSC | Forest Stewardship Council |
| FTA | Free Trade Agreement |
| FTAA | Free Trade Area of the Americas |
| IADB | Inter-American Development Bank |
| ICE | Immigration and Customs Enforcement |
| ICT | Information Communication Technology |
| IHSI | Institut haïtien de statistique et d'informatique |
| ILO | International Labor Organization |
| INEA | National Institute of Adult Education |
| INEGI | Instituto Nacional de Estadística y Geografía |
| INSEE | National Institute of Statistics and Economic Studies |
| INSEE-TER | Institut national de la statistique et des études économiques. Tableaux économiques régionaux |
| IOM | International Organization for Migration |
| ITC | Information Technology of Communication |
| LAFTA | Latin American Free Trade Agreement |
| LGBTI | lesbian, gay, bisexual, transgender, transgender, and intersex |
| MDES | Mouvement de décolonisation, d'émancipation économique et social |
| MERCOSUR | Common Market of the Southern Cone |
| MILA | Integrated Latin American Market |
| MINUSTAH | United Nations Stabilization Mission in Haiti |
| MINVU | Ministry of Housing and Urban Development |

| | |
|---|---|
| NAFTA | North American Free Trade Agreement |
| OECD | Organization for Economic Cooperation and Development |
| OIT | Organization International del Trabajo (or in English, ILO) |
| ORSTOM | Office de la recherche scientifique et technique outre-mer |
| PA | Pacific Alliance |
| PACS | The civil solidarity pact (the official name for the French's same-sex marriage) |
| PDALPD | Le plan départemental d'action pour le logement des personnes défavorisées |
| POS | Plan d'occupation de sol (or in English, land use plan) |
| PRBC18 | 18 Plans for Reconstruction of Coastal Areas |
| PRES | Strategic Sustainable Plans |
| PRONIM | Basic Education Program for Children of Agricultural Migrant Families |
| PRU | Urban Regeneration Plans |
| PSG | Guyanese Socialist Party (in English) |
| PUD | Plan d'aménagement directeur |
| RAFC | Revolutionary Armed Forces of Colombia |
| RSCAS | Centre for Advanced Studies Research |
| SCOT | Schema of Territorial Coherence |
| SDAU | Schéma d'aménagement urbain |
| SESNSP | Executive Secretariat of the National System of Public Security |
| SIGUI | A para-statal housing agency in French Guyana (or in French, Société immobilière de Guyane) |
| TNCA | Northern Triangle of Central America |
| TPP | Trans-Pacific Partnership |
| TTIP | Transatlantic Trade and Investment Partnership |
| UN-MDG | United Nations Millennium Development Goals |
| UNASUR | Union of South American Nations |

| UNESCO | United Nations Educational, Scientific and Cultural Organization |
| UNHCR | United Nations High Commission for Refugees |
| WTO | World Trade Organization |

# LIST OF MAPS

# PROLOGUE[1]

## Areytos for the Shipwrecked: Re/Vuelta

The agaves, the passion fruit that enveloped me,
the silver earmarked for markets beyond

these tropics, they compel you to post outfits at the foot of my bed.
Each morning you blitzkrieg the tavern and pineapple conucos,

---

[1]  I decide to put in my book a poem (in the prologue) authored by the Caribbean and Latin American literature professor, Vincent Toro of New Jersey City University (NJCU). Professor V. Toro declaimed the above poem in the introduction of the third day of the annual colloquium of the department of Latin American and Caribbean Studies-LATI at NJCU.

As one of the keynote speakers of the NJCU 2021 LATI annual Colloquium on Thursday, April 1, 2021 (at 2:00 p.m.), I very much like the poem declaimed by Professor Vincent Toro and asked him to put it in the prologue of my book as a means of keeping the emotional connection, establishing settings, and giving some backgrounds to the readers of my book.

Professor Toro very kindly accepted to give it to me. I wholeheartedly thank him very much for his beautiful poem, which concords perfectly (to some extent) with both the situation of many Latin American and Caribbean immigrants in the United States and with the broader context of the Americas' economic regionalization-globalization.

Once again, I thank you, Professor Toro, for your courtesy. I appreciate it. I am so grateful to you.

Cordially,
Romanovski Zéphirin, PhD

turn the rivers into arsenic, lock my kin up in sheet metal factories,
committing autopsies on their bodies while they are still alive.

You ask me to leave. You ask me to return, mounting electrified
fences around my springs and mineral deposits. You bottle up

the reservoir of my birth and ask me to pay, but I have no currency.
You cut the Aymara, the Quechua, the Lokono from my uvula, pry

me from the vines that nursed me, relocate me to a fiberglass asylum.
Tell me to leave my farm fallow. Indict me when I protest,

when I beg to be buried next to my mother. You ask me to leave.
You ask me to return. You irrigate my daughter's veins, widow

me with your excavations, post eviction notices on my hearth
and render me a vagrant in my own roost. When I scale

the Andes to nest in the backyard of your vacation home,
you drop the red flag and cry encroachment. With a single

papaya I then camp beneath a bridge, lay a blanket across
your metropolis of dismembered mainframes. You send

subpoenas, coin me trespasser. You ask me to return, you ask me to
leave, demand I make myself useful if I am to stay. I repair

your appliances, put up drywall, pick your apples, polish your porce-
lain, raise your kids who never see you because you are in

my country putting up luxury townhouses, carving my cousins into
chattel. From your detritus I harvest a new family, subsisting

on only prayer and memory. Feed my kids tomes you abandon in
landfills until they siphon the venom from your syntax,

miracle your numerals, and earn a seat in the academy next to your
offspring. Now you demand a refund on what

you stole. You stifle me after I unearth your cooked books,
smear me for dismantling the guillotine circus you pitch

on my stoop, then dispatch an assistant to offer a settlement of rotten
tripe. When I show you a deed to the land, you

mispronounce my name. You create a shortage of spikenard.
Invent the idea of *North*. You hock haute couture coups.

Make a lullaby of my wounds. Then you ask me to leave.
You ask me to return. To return. To leave. To return. To

leave. To return. To. To. Turn. To.    To leave.    To.
    To. To. To.    To. Deceive.            To.


             To. To leave.
To. To.            To. To.
                You ask me. To.
                    To leave.
To re.            To turn.


To receive.            You ask.
        Me.        You ask.
Me to
      believe.
                To re.
To. turn.
      To. To. To. To. To. To. To. To. To. To.


    (Vincent Toro)

# 1

# Introduction: Shifting from Politics to Economic Logics in Globalization as Political Geography and Geopolitics in the Americas

## Abstract

The interplay of state, historical economic development policies, power, and space issues drives political geography and geopolitics as consequential to globalization in the Americas through migration and network cities. The interconnected networks of mobility of human, capital, goods, and information influxes across borders transform and link scattered spaces at various geographical scales.

People who are circulating, working, and living in diverse scales of spaces raise the issues of territorial governance, politics of scales, political geography, and geopolitics within the liberalized free-trade zones in the globalized-regionalized Americas.

Geopolitics of globalization cannot be simply reduced to the traditional political sphere of influence and military alliances to protect some economic interests.

As a result, the articulation of problematical, methodological, and theoretical elements reveals the key role of free-trade arrangements, capital, and human mobility across borders and, to a lesser extent, the impact of the use of natural resources and the official discourse on economic liberalization. These parameters are the reasons explaining the shift from political and security rationales to geoeconomics as geopolitics of globalization in the Americas.

Keywords: globalization, economic integration, migration, cities, geopolitics, geo-sociology, transnationalism, Latin America, and the Americas.

Globalization[2] shows that geopolitics[3] shifts overtime from the traditional dominant diplomacy-security rationale to more hegemonic geoeconomics[4] drivers.

---

[2] *Globalization* refers to the integrated flows of social, economic, information, and spatial networks.

Also, "Globalization centres on compression of the world economy undermining the sovereignty of the nation state and shifting power to nonstate forces encompassing inter-governmental, non-governmental, and private institutions which increasingly shape and steer policies" (Walton and Roy 2012, 3).

Additionally, Sparke (2014, 24) who refers to Held (1999) writes that

> Perhaps the most exhaustive examination available defines globalization thus in terms of the extension, acceleration and intensification of consequential worldwide interconnections (Held, et al 1999). […]…if globalization is conceptualized as the widening, deepening and speeding up of global interconnectedness (Held, et al, 1999: 14), it is also possible to pick it apart as a process which embodies a transformation in the spatial organization of social relations and transactions assessed in terms of their extensity, intensity, velocity and impact generating transcontinental or interregional flows and networks of activity, interaction and the exercise of power. (Held et al, 1999, 16)

[3] Briefly, the term *geopolitics* refers to the relationship of states, power, and space. Very largely, geopolitics was developed in the context of colonialism and imperialism. Valdivieso (2018) citing O'Tuathail defines *geopolitics* as "the study of spatialization of international politics by core powers and hegemonic states." Geopolitics is no longer "state-centric." Instead, geopolitics crosses the global scale to reach the local scale through the major concept of spatialization that includes broad topics within the critical geography approach (Valdivieso 2018).

[4] Mercille (2008, 576) wrote that

> The term geoeconomics has been used to described the alleged dominance of economics over politics in

Aside from the colonial past, the political regionalization of the Americas can be traced back through the independence in the nineteenth and early twentieth centuries. The contextualization offers an important historical parameter to understand the early twenty-first century globalization as an object of contemporary geopolitics.

Generally speaking, the emergence of the United States as the hegemonic power, the strategy of containment of communism in the second half of the twentieth century, and by the end of the twentieth century, the economic liberalization-regionalization through integrative regional and subregional bodies and the shift in economic development policy approaches (import-substitution/export-oriented economy) marked to some degree not only the regional political geography, but also, more importantly, some changes in geopolitical calculus and practices of many Western Hemisphere national governments.

If the contextualization briefly mentions the historical geographical formation of the region through the United States'[5] dominant

---

interstates relations in recent years (Luttwak 1993), the unevenness of the global economy (Dicken 2003) and European integration (Pollard and Sidaway 2002). In general, geographers, have conceived of geoeconomics in at least three ways: first, as referring to the natural resources contained within a region and the politics of controlling and exploiting such resources (e.g., O' Hara and Hefferman 2006); second as discourse closely linked to the economic imperatives of the global economy (Smith 2002; Sparke 2002,217, 2017; Toal 1997); and third, to point to the flows of trade, finance and capital over global space and across borders, taking into consideration the political aspects behind such movements. (Agnew and Corbridge 1989; Coleman 2005; Corbridge and Agnew 1991; Sidaway 2005; Smith 2003)

[5] The James Monroe Doctrine in 1823 in US foreign policy prevents former colonial European powers that any incursion in the Americas will be considered as an attack against the United States. But in 1905, former president Theodore Roosevelt largely started using the Monroe Doctrine to establish its domination (as an imperialist country) on the whole Americas as a geographical region. As

political, security, and economic actions for political geographical analysis, it also mainly focuses on state, power, and space, expressing the contemporary geopolitics of the Americas as the process of economic globalization enfolds.

Globalization is portrayed as a shift in regional-global geopolitics,[6] where transnational economic factors and actors outclass traditional political and security rationales in shaping politics, policy,

---

a matter of fact, the Monroe Doctrine became a geopolitical doctrine in the political geography of the Americas.

[6] Norton (2007, 311 312) defines *geopolitics* as "the study of relevance of space and distance to questions of international relations." The author emphasizes on key variables of location and physical environment to explain "world power distribution" or "global distribution of power."

Furthermore, as geoeconomics becomes the dominant dimension of geopolitics in the era of globalization, the book (from the early 1990s to date) underlines the geopolitics evolution, in addition to security issues, state power, and politics, to encompass economic integration, development, globalization and global issues.

Generally speaking, geopolitics is often the pretext of instrumenting geography to pursue an internal/external political agenda.

For his part, Philip Kithome (2020) focuses on the historical and conceptual evolution of geopolitics.

> Geopolitics has a lengthy and varied history on the twentieth century and has moved beyond its original meaning to signify the general concern with politics and geography. Coming up with a meaning for geopolitics is difficult as it seems to change as historical eras and structure of the world order evolves... The imperialist thinkers understood the term [geopolitics] as the part of western imperial knowledge that was concerned with the relationship between the physical earth and politics... [During the Cold War] The former secretary of state, Henry Kissinger revived the term [geopolitics] by using it to refer to the game of balance of power politics that takes place across the global political map. (Toal et al. 1998, 2)

> Geopolitics is popular because it handles the comprehensive visions of the global political map. It looks at the bigger picture and avails ways of relating the local and regional dynamics to the global system at large.

and legislative agendas of national states. In other words, globalization problematized as geopolitics underlines the primacy of liberal capitalist corporation in controlling territories by undermining, to some extent, the traditional "sacrosanct" absolute sovereignty of the national states and by abandoning some key statal prerogatives to transnational corporations and big firms as a matter of a new liberal political geography and geopolitics operatives in the post-Cold War new liberal interdependent geoeconomics acting as new geopolitics of "territorial expansion of capitalism" (Harvey 1885).

Once again, the problematization of globalization and geopolitics[7] (Sparke 2014) does not neglect the weight of the old politi-

---

> Geopolitics is also of interest to some people as it holds a promise to the insightful direction of the international affairs and the shaping of the world's political map. (Toal et al. 1998, 3)

> It has a multidimensional global cachet hence it promotes a spatial way of thinking. (Kithome 2020, 2)

[7] The post-Cold War geopolitics corresponds to what Sparke (2014, 2020) describes as

> The assertive framing power of globalization discourse has been especially obvious (and obscuring) is in international relations and associated diplomatic, military, and foreign policy discussions that frame war, peace and security in the terms of, on the one side, disconnection and geopolitical danger, and, on the other, global integration and geoeconomic opportunity (Dalby, 2010; Roberts et al, 2003; Essex, 2013; Morrissey, 2009 & 2011;Sparke, 2007).

> In place of orthodox geopolitics and its concerns for soldiers and citizens, this geoeconomic grammar tends to elevate the entrepreneurial interests of investors and customers; in contrast to a geopolitical focus on national borders and place, it privileges networks and pace; and instead of concentrating international politics on building alliances for "security" against supposed "evil empires," geoeconomics is primarily concerned with

cal and security dimensions of geopolitics, which obviously play an important role in the internally and externally distribution of population, spatialization (urban-rural) of social life, and socio-spatial structures impacting interstate relations and foreign policy of the containment strategy to fight communism in the Americas.

The connection between the old[8] Cold War and the post-Cold War geopolitics[9] (Dominguez 1989) is valued, and more impor-

---

> building international partnerships that advance "growth,"
> "integration," "harmonization," and "efficiency," against the
> threats of "traditionalism," "isolationism," "anachronism"
> and "anarchy." (Sparke, 2020: 35)

[8] Old or "orthodox" geopolitics described above by Sparke (2014, 35) as "concerns for soldiers and citizens."

[9] In referring to the work of Dominguez (1989), the Americas' shift in geopolitics, which can be explained by the attempt to pacify violent conflicts, promote peace, security, democracy, and prosperity. The Western hemisphere moves from the old "*Cold War*" geopolitics (1960–1990) with "the internal mission for the army"—to the post-Cold War after 1991 [which is] "torn by the security dilemma" between "internal and/or external mission for the armies" in the context of economic liberalization and integration (Dominguez 1989).

Dominguez (1989, 6, 7) noted that in the 1990s, the region experienced "some civilian governments eschewed assigning internal mission to the armed forces if such could be avoided... The principal remaining option to safeguard domestic stability was to assign external missions to the armed forces: my neighbor may be my enemy."

Also, in the post-Cold War, particularly in the first half of the 1990s, aside from the traditional political preoccupations of the armed forces in terms of protecting politico-institutional stability and elected democratic governance, as stated by Dominguez (1989,) there was "a shift from external assignments to the army to a more internal role." That change has its "internal and its external political consequences" (military influence and possible coups). Some new challenges impact local-national and external politics and policy. The issues are, very briefly, military and guerilla demobilization, gang violence, drug trafficking posing a threat for domestic stability. Generally, the consequences are transborder problems affecting more than one state. As a result, the post-Cold War in the Americas saw the rise in security cooperation and the role of supranational bodies to coordinate security matters and keep peace and public order in the region, which adopts very largely institutional democracy as a mode of government of the states engaging in economic regionalization and integration.

tantly, the new one constitutes the main object of the book as portrayed above.

Additionally, economic regionalization-globalization ties migration flows, migrants' trajectories, and routes to show how the current geoeconomics[10] of the post-Cold War geopolitics of the globalization in the Americas creates historical ethno-demographic conditions to form, for example, a Caribbean diaspora in connection to the United States in Florida (Portes and Grosfoguel 1994). The new geopolitics of globalization inherited some population-migration mobility patterns in urban-rural areas in both origin and host countries. In other words, the book tends to point out, to some extent, the interconnection of diverse spaces and places through historical population movements and distribution in cities, urban-rural landscape production, territory, territoriality, and transnationality in the Americas. All these elements relate to (to some extent) a continuum in rationales of

---

[10] Sparke (2014, 10, 11), who also departed the use of the concept of geoeconomics from Edward Luttwak (1993) to explain the interstate competition within globalization, also extended its meaning to cover the way people view the map of the global political economy. This extension in the sense of the concept allows Sparke (2014, 10, 11) to reinforce his view by citing Sklair (2001, 127) about the term *geoeconomics* as a matter of geopolitics.

So Sparke (2014, 11) wrote that

> "Boundary less behavior," enthuses the report, involves "behavior that tramples or demolishes all barriers of rank, function, geography, and bureaucracy in an endless pursuit of the best idea in the cause of engaging and involving every mind in the company." (quoted in Sklair 2001, 127)

> Technological and regulatory developments in the world economy have created a "global surface" on which a dominant organisational form [the global corporation] will develop and inexorably wipe out less efficient competitors who are no longer protected by national or local barriers. Such an organisation, it is argued is place-less and boundary-less."

past and present geopolitics[11] (Flint and Taylor 2011, 33, 65, 66, 67) resulting of state, power, and space relationship in the capitalist control over scales of territories and the use of natural resources in the Americas as a region shaped by various integrated phases of regionalization and hegemony of the United States's political, security, and economic (influences) agendas.

---

[11]

Geopolitics was the study, some claimed science, of explaining and predicting the strategic behavior of states. States were the exclusive agents of geopolitics. And deciding state actions was seen as a form of politics almost exclusively dominated by men, hence the term statemen. But, the contemporary understanding of geopolitics is much different indeed one set of definitions would classify all politics as geopolitics in a broad understanding that no conflict is separate from its spatial setting. (Flint and Taylor 2011, 65)

The geographical entities of place, space, scale, region, network and territory will be introduced and used to define geopolitics.

The interaction between structure and agency, and power will be used to understand geopolitics. (Flint and Taylor 2011, 33)

The ideas of structure and agency are part of an intellectual debate within social science that can get us into some very complex philosophy. My goal here is to provide enough material for you to interpret contemporary geopolitics, rather than negotiating the philosophical debate… A structure is a set of rules (formal as in legally enforceable laws) and norms (culturally accepted practices) that partially determine what can and cannot, could and should not, be done. In this sense, structures are expressions of power as they define what is permissible and expected. Agents are those entities attempting to act. (Flint and Taylor 2011, 66, 67)

As the dominant global "structural power"[12] (Kitchen and Cox 2019) the United States, by putting forth economic region-

---

[12] Among other conceptual and theoretical tools used to analyze the geopolitics of globalization, the book, in an international relations and diplomacy perspective, underlines the shift in power literature and practice through the difference between "relational power" defined in terms of "states capabilities" and "structural power" (Kitchen and Cox 2019).

While the "relational power" is evoked in the analysis, the concept of "structural power" is largely employed to highlight the international relations and the geopolitics of globalization.

> Structural power…describes the balance of advantage built into systems of states' interaction. We argue that it is structural power—not relational capabilities—that is determining of international leadership…and change international order. (Kitchen and Cox 2019, 2)

> We review the concept of structural power and show how ideological and technological developments in the international system in the 20th century, both render structural advantages more significant to questions of international leadership than the balance of relative national capabilities, and mitigate against systemic changes that might bring strength and structural position into greater alignment. (Kitchen and Cox 2019, 2)

> In the discipline of international relations, structural power has become primarily associated with Susan Strange's image of a four-sided pyramid of structural power, in which the four planes—the production, finance, security and knowledge structures—hold each other in place. (Strange 2015)

"Structural power" and "relational power" are theoretically differed to one another in international relations. However, under some circumstances and in practice, they are self-fertilizing, particularly in analyzing the remaking of the international order in the context of globalization and the unipolar world of the post-Cold War.

"Structural power persists, where relative capabilities may wax and wane, because opportunities for comprehensively remaking international order and reconfiguring the allocation of this type of institutional or agenda setting' power are rate" (Kitchen and Cox 2019, 9).

alization-globalization in its international relations and diplomacy (Gilpin 1987, Kerr and Wiseman 2018), continues to maintain its hegemony, extending its dominance in different ways in the Americas and worldwide, while developing a "retrenchment strategy"[13] (Stokes and Waterman 2017).

Moreover, labor migration is seen as a corollary of global economic liberalization and integration. The factor of migrant workers is an essential theoretical assumption of migrant network (Massey 1987, Krissman 2005) and, to some extent, labor migrant from periphery countries to global cities in the global economy (Sassen 1991, Brenner and Theodore 2005). However, if labor migrant and migrant network at the beginning (and on the short-term) are dependent on economic liberalization and globalization in global cities and go together with a certain type of international politics and geopolitics on the long-term where migrant workers and international migrant network processes become interconnected one to another on transnationalized network geographical loci (Zéphirin 2016, 2017, 2018).

Obviously, problematizing geopolitics as geoeconomics of the globalization[14] raises some problematic questions (Luttwak 1993; Mercille 2008; Sparke 2014, 29).

---

[13] As a matter of fact, the "retrenchment strategy" proposed by Stokes and Waterman (2017) in international relations (goes along with the US "grand strategy"), added to economic regionalization-globalization, represents a form to keep the US hegemony running without military interventions in the Americas and, more importantly, in other major world regions too often. In other words, the concept of "structural power," theoretically and practically, interlaces the United States hegemony and its "retrenchment strategy" (Stokes and Waterman 2017). Retrenchment appears to be an alternative to avoid worldwide frequent direct and costly military interventions.

[14]

Globalization as a term therefore also distinguishes the current post-Fordist, post Cold War era of market liberalization in which transnational corporations have increasingly moved from balancing mass production and mass consumption nationally to pursue market opportunities globally. All the ideas about inevitability and leveling have undoubtedly helped business leaders make

How to evaluate the significance of globalization to transnational migrations in network cities and rural territories producing politics of scale and a geo-sociology, revisiting geopolitics in the Americas, and more importantly, what are the development policy implications?

Beyond the empirical evaluation of free-trade areas and labor market liberalization, what is the theoretical underpinning of the geopolitics of globalization, the politics of scale, and the geo-sociology, and more importantly, how to do research and test hypotheses on transnational migrations and globalized network cities in the Americas?

In order to answer the above research-guided questions, first, the book posits that the geopolitics of globalization sparks a geo-sociology and politics of scales, shaping political geography and internal-external politics and policies through the causes and effects of free-trade areas, transnational migrations, human settlement patterns, ethnocultural and demographic changes, city growth, and urban governance.

Second, the book states that the economic liberalization rationales give way little by little to new politics of scale, political geographies, and geopolitics engendered by the self-produced interconnected migrant network, international migration network, and reversible migration processes crossing national borders of integrative economic bodies in their combined diverse causes and effects. In other words, all these are new parameters and problematic elements to rethink from global-regional to local geographical scales the geopolitics[15] of globalization through migration in network cities in the Americas.

---

the political case for neoliberal policies around the world and they have also led to the rethinking of international relations and geopolitics in terms of geoeconomics, but neoliberalization and the shock doctrines of market reform have also engendered many diverse forms of global resistance too. (Sparke 2014, 29)

[15] Methodologically, in reference to the use of human geography concepts to "investigate geopolitics" by Flint and Taylor (2011, 33, 63), the book interconnects "geographical entities" (previously mentioned) with the social

Specifically, the book aims at analyzing the geoeconomics of globalization and its theoretical implications for geo-sociology and politics of scales through economic integrative arrangements, transnational migration flows, city growth, and urban governance as a matter of political geography and critical geopolitics in the Americas.

Generally, the book purposes to show through the broader theoretical perspectives of political geography and critical geopolitics (also radical geopolitics) the important role played by the geoeconomics and the political economy theory in international relations to shape power, policy, and space in the Americas (Gilpin 1987; Malawer 1988; Harvey 1985, 2001; O'Tuathhail, Dodds, and Sidaway 1994; Barton 2003; Mercille 2008; Mamadouh and Muller 2017; Agnew 2005; Agnew and Corbridge 1995; Moisio 2019).

In this view, the book explores diverse theoretical contributions such as the political economy theory as an element of critical geography, the world-economy theory (Wallerstein 2004), migrant network and international migration network (Massey et al. 1987, Krissman 2005, Zéphirin 2005, Zéphirin 2018), the inter-American migration system (Smith 2001, Zéphirin 2016), and network cities and global cities (Sassen 1991, Dupuis 1997, Castells 1996).

Also, even the David Harvey (2001a, 2001b) theory of "two logics of power" and "spatial fix" explaining the territorial expansion of capitalism neglects to some degree the political dimension of the geoeconomics (Mercille 2008, 570–586) related to the globalization.

In a methodological standpoint, the book, in analyzing the geoeconomics as a matter of critical geopolitics of globalization, takes account secondarily of the factors of natural resources and the offi-

---

structuration theory (structure and agency) in social sciences, among other theories, to elucidate the geopolitics of globalization. The geopolitical agents are involved in the making of geopolitics by acting in main structures of globalization bodies creating laws, norms, power, and advantages.

A provisional list of geopolitical agents could include: individuals, households, protest groups, countries, corporations, NGO's, political parties, rebel groups, and organized labor, though this list is far from complete. Similar to our discussion of geographic scale, it follows that these agents are not separate but entwined. (Flint and Taylor 2011, 66)

cial discourse on economic liberalization while primarily focuses its problematic attention and argumentations on the constitution of economic integrative bodies, flows of trade and capital investments, human mobility across borders, and the politics and policy behind these processes (Harvey 1985, 2001a, 2006; Mercille 2008, 576). As a matter of fact, the book uses various sources of quantitative data and literature review to develop its argumentations on the geopolitics of globalization affecting transnational migration in network cities in the Americas.

Definitely, all the conceptual, theoretical, and methodological instruments mobilized to structure the argumentations of the book reverberate in the five chapters that are underlined below.

The first chapter revisits developments in political geography and geopolitics as consequential to globalization in the Americas through migration and network cities. The interconnected networks caused by the mobility of human, capital, goods, and information influxes across borders transform and link scattered spaces at various geographical scales. Local, national, and regional displacements of people who look for a better living transnationalize rural and urban territories by connecting one to another. The combined causes and effects of human mobility and settlement types for various purposes in transnational network loci in the Americas show new evidences to revisit the geopolitics in the light of globalization.

As a matter of fact, the first chapter lays the methodological and conceptual foundations to analyze the interplay of geopolitics and globalization in the Americas as a region. The regionalization process portrays the historical context and the theoretical approaches used to structure the argumentation of the book and explain the geopolitical shift in as a means of globalization.

The second chapter describes and analyzes the general and overall states of affairs. It focuses on the impact of globalization on labor markets, emigration (push), immigration (pull) factors, wherein the return migration flows. The chapter undertakes to describe the effects of globalization in its many forms and at the overall regional level, affecting economies and societies in Latin American nations. In fact, this chapter federates and summarizes the different elements and raises the whole problematic context of a geo-sociology of globalization and its significance. Consequently, the chapter emphasizes on the interface of practical and theoretical dimensions that concern various actors on various geographical scales involving diverse activities in the region and evaluate whether the geo-sociology of globalization works to the advantage or the disadvantage of migrants, while comparing south-north and south-south migrations in the Americas.

Also, in a more specific manner, the third chapter addresses the mobility of labor, capital, and human beings in residences between Haiti and French Guyana. In this view, the Haitian-French Guyanese migration, with its multipolar interactions, becomes a subsystem of the inter-American migration space. And the conjunction of emigration, immigration and return migration in their interrelated causes and effects drives a geo-sociology, politics of scale, political geographies, and geopolitics in Latin American globalization.

The regional space of economic production in which transnational migrants and transnational corporation are involved raises the need for economic blocs in Latin America to overcome their overt competition as a path for cooperation in the globalization.

Furthermore, the fourth chapter moves from an evaluative problematic perspective of migration, cities, globalization, and geopolitics to elevate the subject on a theoretical level. The fourth chapter explores the interplay of a clearly specified theoretical framework to understand and explain grounded evidences making the geopolitics and the geo-sociology of globalization. This chapter not only develops, explains, and articulates different theoretical contributions that highlight key issues in detail, but more importantly, it returns on and sheds lights on practical, theoretical, and epistemic concerns in doing research and producing new and updated knowledge in the Americas' geopolitics as an understanding of migration, cities, and globalization.

Additionally, the fifth chapter returns to precedent sections of the book and, more broadly, merges the theoretical and conceptual tools related to geopolitics of globalization and the implications for migration and network cities in the Americas.

This chapter intersects the theoretical lenses of political geography, critical geography, social constructivism, deconstructivism, and international relations theories to explain the shift from the traditional geopolitics to the liberal geoeconomics as a new type of geopolitics related to the complex interdependence within the capitalist economic regionalization-globalization (Agnew and Corbridge 1989; Agnew and Corbridge 1995; Agnew 2003, 2005; Moisio 2019; Arrighi 1994; Wallerstein 1998; O'Thuathail 1996; Derida 1994, 1998).

In fact, this chapter interacts practices and theories of economic regionalization, state power structures, transnational human mobility, and urban-rural settlement patterns as a matter of political geography and geopolitics.

In other words, the chapter refers to power structures in interstate relations as consequential to space-state-power formation and national development policy in the inter-American region through different historical periods to both understand and explain in a rupture and continuity logic the evolution and the outclassed traditional geopolitics by the newly predominant geoeconomics in the globalization as a new geopolitics in the Americas. As a result, the different actors involved in the globalization point out significant changes in space, spatialization, regionalization, political geography, and geopolitics.

Finally, all the above chapters of the book are blended and crossed in part or in whole by the thematic connecting lines of migration, cities, economic integration, geo-sociology, politics of scale, and political geographies in order to explain the geopolitics of globalization in the Americas.

# References


Agnew, J. 2003. *Geopolitics: Re-visioning World Politics* (2nd ed.). London: Routledge.

Agnew, J. 2005. *Hegemony: The New Shape of Global Power.* Philadelphia: Temple University Press.

Agnew, J. and S. Corbridge. 1989. "The New Geopolitics: The Dynamics of Geopolitical Disorder." In R. Johnson and P. Taylor (eds.). *The World in Crisis: Geographical Perspectives* (2nd ed.) Oxford: Basil Blackwell.

Agnew, J. A. and J. Corbridge. 1995. *Mastering Space. Hegemony, Territory and International Political Economy.* London: Routledge.

Agnew, J. 1994. "The Territorial Trap: The Geographical Assumptions of International Relations Theory." *Review of International Political Economy* 1:53–80.

Agnew, J. 1998. "Mapping Political Power Beyond State Boundaries: Territory, Identity and Movement in World Politics." *Millennium* 28 no. 3: 499–521.

Arrighi, G. 1994. *The Long Twentieth Century.* London: Verso.

Campbell, D. 1992. *Writing Security: United States Foreign Policy and The Politics of Identity.* Minneapolis: University of Minnesota Press.

Barton, R. Jonathan. 2003. *A Political Geography of Latin America.* Taylor and Francis, eBook: London.

Budd, L. 1998. "Territorial Competition and Globalisation: Scylla and Charybdis of European cities." *Urban Studies* 35: 663–686.

Brenner, N., B., Jessop, Jones, G., MacLeod. 2003. "State Space in Question." In *State/Space: A Reader.* Oxford: Blackwell.

Brenner, N. and N. Theodore. 2005. Neoliberalism and the Urban Condition. *City*, 9: 101–106. https://doi.org/10.1080/13604810500092106.

Choais, Françoise. 2014. *Urbanisme, Utopies et Réalités.* Paris: Seuil.

Castells, M. 1983. *The City and the Grassroots: A Cross-Cultural Theory of Urban Social Movement.* Berkeley: University of California Press.

Castells, M. 1996. *The Rise of the Network Society.* Oxford: Blackwell.

Carling, J. and L. F. Collins. 2007. "Aspiration, Desire and Drivers of Migration." Routledge: Taylor and Francis.

Coleman, M. 2005. "US Statecraft and the US-Mexico Border as Security/Economy Nexus." *Political Geography*, 24 (2): 189–205.

Corbridge, S. and J. Agnew. 1991. *The US Trade and Budget Deficits in Global Perspective: An Essay in Geopolitical Economy.* Environment and Planning D: Society and Space 9:71–90.

Cosma, Sorinel. 2010. Immanuel Wallerstein's World-System Theory. Ovidius Universitaty Constanta, Facultaty of Economic Sciences: 221–224.

Dicken, P. 2003. *Global Shift: Reshaping the Global Economic Map in the 21st Century* (4th ed). New York: Guilford.

Dalby, S. 2007. "Regions, Strategies and Empire in the Global War on Terror." *Geopolitics* 12 (14): 586–606.

Deacon, Roger. 2006. "Michel Foucault on Education: A Preliminary Theoretical Overview." South African Journal of Education, vol. 26 (2):177–187.

Derida, Jacques. 1994. *Specters of Marx: The State of the Debt, the Work of Morning and the New International.* (Transl. Peggy Kamuf) New York: Routledge.

Derida, Jacques. 1998. *Of Grammatology* (Transl. Gayatri Chakravorty Spivak). Connected Edition. Baltimore: The John Hopkins University Press.

Dodds, J. K. and J. Sidaway. 1994. "Locating Critical Geopolitics." *Environment and Planning D.* Society and Space 12:515–524.

Dominguez, I. Jorge. 1998. "Security, Peace and Democracy in Latin America and the Caribbean: Challenges for the Post-Cold War Era." In *International Security and Democracy. Latin America and the Caribbean in the Post-Cold War Era.* Pittsburgh: University of Pittsburgh Press.

Dupuis, Gabriel. 1991. *L'urbanisme des réseaux—Théories et méthodes.* Paris: Armand Colin.

Ellis, R. Evan. 2013. "China's Growing Relationship with Latin America and the Caribbean in the Context of US Policy Toward the Region." In *Air and Space Power Journal*: 1–15.

Ellis, R. Evan. 2015. *China's Activities in the Americas. Testimony to the Joint Hearing of the Subcommittee on the Western Hemisphere.* Foreign Affairs Committee, US House of Representatives. Washington.

Ellis, R. Evan. 2017. "The Strategic Context of China's Advance in Latin America: An Update." In *Note: Observatoire Chine 2017/2018.*

Flint, Colin. and J. Peter Taylor. 2011. *Political Geography: World-Economy, Nation-State, and Locality* (6th ed.). Harlow: Prentice-Hall.

Flint, Colin and Peter Taylor. 2018. *Political Geography: World Geography, Nation-State and Locality* (7th ed.). Routledge.

Gallager, P. Kevin. 2016. *The China Triangle: Latin America's China Boom and the Fate of the Washington Consensus* (1st ed.). Oxford University Press.

Giddens, A. 1985. *The Nation-State and Violence.* Cambridge: Polity.

Gilpin, Robert. 1987. *The Political Economy of International Relations.* Princeton, NJ: Princeton University Press.

Guzzini, Stephano. 2005. "The Concept of Power: A Constructivist Analysis." *Millenium Journal of International Studies* 33 (3): 495–521.

Fukuyama, Francis. 1992. *The End of History and the Last Man.* Hamondsworth: Penguin.

Harvey, David. 1985. "The Geopolitics of Capitalism." In D. Gregory and D. Urry (eds.) *Social Relations and Spatial Structures.* London: MacMillan. 128–163.

Harvey, David. 2001a. "Globalization and the Spatial Fix." *Geographische Revue* 2:23–30.

Harvey, David. 2001b. *Spaces of Capital: Toward a Critical Geography.* New York: Routledge.

Harvey, David. 2003. *The New Imperialism.* Oxford: Oxford University Press.

Harvey, David. 2006. *Spaces of Global Capitalism. Towards a Theory of Uneven Geographical Development.* London: Verso.

Kelly, P. 2006. "A Critique of Critical Geopolitics." *Geopolitics* 11 (1): 24–53.

Kerr, Pauline and Geoffrey Wiseman. 2018. *Diplomacy in a Globalizing World: Theories and Practices.* Second Edition. Oxford: Oxford University Press.

Keoahane, Robert O. and Joseph S. Nye. 1987. "Power and Interdependence Revisited." *International Organization* 41:725–753.

Kitchen, Nicholas and Michael Cox. 2019. "Power, Structural Power, and American Decline." www.http//.reprints.lse.ac.uk.

Kithome, Philip. 2020. *Geopolitics—First Name Last Name Institution.* Academia: 1–12. Order: 207 (3). docx Online. Paper.

Krissman, Fred. 2005. "Sin Coyote ni Patron: Why the Migrant Network Fails to Explain International Migration." *International Migration Review (IMR)* 39, no. 1 (Spring): 4–44.

Lacoste, Y. 1985. *La géographie ça sert d'abord à faire la guerre.* 2ieme édition. Paris: (FM) La Decouverte.

Lefebvre, H. 1977. *De l'Etat: le mode de production étatique* (vol. 3). Paris: Union Générale d'Editions.

Lefebvre, H. 1978. *De l'Etat: les contradictions de l'Etat moderne* (vol. 4). Paris: Union Génerale d'Editions.

Lefebvre, H. 1991. *The Production of Space.* Oxford: Blackwell.

Luttwak, E. 1993. *The Endangered American Dream.* New York: Simon and Schuster.

Lebedeva, Alexandra and Lopez Mercedes-Maria. 2014. *The Construction of Immigrants' Identity in the EU. A Foucauldian Discourse Analysis of EU Common Migratory Policy.* Umca University.

Malawer, S. Stuart. 1988. "The Political Economy of International Relations by Robert Gilpin." In *Maryland Journal of International Law,* vol.12, issue 2, article 6: 307–311.

Mammadouh, V. 1998. "Geopolitics in the Nineties: One Flag Many Meanings." *GeoJournal* 46: 237–253.

Mamadouh, V. and M. Muller. 2017. "Political Geography and Geopolitics." In *European Regions and Boundaries. A Conceptual History.* Diana Mishkova and Balazs Trencsenyi: 259–279. New York: Berghahan.

Mercille, Julien. 2008. "The Radical Geopolitics of US Foreign Policy Geopolitical and Geoeconomic Logic of Power." *Political Geography Elsevier,* vol. 27: 570–586.

Massey, S. Douglas et al. 1987. *Return to Aztlan: The Social Process of International Migration from Western Mexico.* Berkeley: University of California.

Massey Douglas S. 1993. "Theories of International Migration." *Population and Development Review* 19, no. 3: 431–466.

McCormick, T. 2004. "World Systems." In M. Hogan and T. Paterson (eds.) *Explaining the American Foreign Relations* (2nd ed.): 149–161.

Moisio, Sami. 2019. Re-Thinking Geoeconomics: Towards a Political Geography of Economic Geographies. *Geography Compass.* 13: e12466. https://doi.org/10.1111/gec3.12466.

Norton, William. 2007. *Human Geography* (sixth edition). New York: Oxford University Press.

O'Hara, S. and M. Hefferman. 2006. "From Geo-strategy to Geoeconomics: The Heartland and the British Imperialism before and after Mackinder." *Geopolitics* 11, no. 1: 54–73.

Oslender, Ulrich. 2016. "*The Geography of Social Movements. Afro-Colombian Mobilization and the Aquatic Space.*" Durham: Duke University Press.

O'Tuathail, Gearoid and J. Agnew. 1998. "Geopolitics and Discourse, Practical Geopolitics Reasoning in American Foreign Policy." *The Geopolitical Reader.* 78–92.

O'Tuathail, Gearoid. 1996. *Critical Geopolitics. The Politics of Writing Global Space.* Minneapolis: University of Minnesota Press.

Pollard, J. and J. Sidaway. 2002. "Nostalgia for the Future: The Geoeconomics and the Geopolitics of the Euro." *Transactions of the Institute of British Geographers,* 27: 518–521.

Pulsipher, Lydia Mihelic and Alex Pulsipher. 2015. *World Regional Geography Concepts* (3rd ed.). New York: W. H. Freeman and Company, Macmillan Education Company.

Puntigliano, A. R. 2016. *21st Century Geopolitics: Integration and Development in the Age of Continental States. Territory, Politics and Governance.* Routledge: Taylor and Francis.

Portes, A. and R. Grosfoguel. 1994. "Caribbean Diasporas: Migration and Ethnic Communities." *The Annals of the American Academy of Political and Social Science* 553: 48–69.

Rivas, Simon. 2020. *Geopolitics. Sine Loco.*

Sassen, Saskia. 1991. *The Global City: New York, London, Tokyo.* Princeton: Princeton University Press.

Sharp, J. 1996. "Hegemony, Popular Culture and Geopolitics: The Reader's Digest and the Construction of Danger." *Political Geography* 11, no. 2: 557–570.

Sidaway, J. 2005. "Asia-Europe-United States: The Geoeconomics of Uncertainty." *Area* 37, no. 4: 373–377.

Smith, William C. and Lora Gomez-Mera. 2010. *Market, State and Society in Contemporary Latin America.* New York: Willey Blackwell.

Smith, A. 2002. "Imagining Geographies of the New Europe: Geoeconomic Power of the New European Architecture of Integration." *Political Geography* 21, no. 5: 647–670.

Soja, E. W. 1989. *Postmodern Geographies: The Reassertion of Space in Critical Social Theory.* London: Verso.

Sparke, M. 2002. "Not a state, but more than a state of mind: cascading cascadias and geoeconomics of cross-border regionalism." In M. Perkmann and N. Sum (eds.). *Globalization, Regionalization, and Cross-Border Regions,* 212–240. London: Palgrave.

Sparke, M. 2007. "Geopolitical Fears, Geoeconomic Hopes. And the Responsibilities of Geography." *Annals of the Association of American Geographers,* 97, no. 2: 337–348.

Sparke, M. 2014. *Defining Globalization: Work in Progress.* University of Washington (Found on Academia Online Research Engine). Draft entry on GLOBALIZATION for *The International Encyclopedia of Geography: People, the Earth, Environment, and Technology,* edited by Douglas Richardson et al, forthcoming from Wiley.

Stokes, Doug and Kit Waterman. 2017. "Security Leverage, Structural Power and US Strategy in East Asia." *International Affairs* 9: 1039–1060. The Royal Institute of International Affairs: *Oxford University Press.*

Taylor, P. 1985. *Political Geography: World Economy, Nation-State and Locality* (1st ed.). London: Longman.

Taylor, P. 1996. *The Way the Modern World Works: World Hegemony to World Impasse.* New York: John Wiley.

Taylor, P. J. 2004. *World City Network: A Global Urban Analysis.* New York: Routledge, Taylor, and Francis Group.

Toal, G., G. O'Tuathail, S. Dalby, and P. Routledge (eds.). 1998. *The Geopolitics Reader.* Psychology Press.

Valdivieso, J. P. 2012. *Understanding Critical Geopolitics. Sine Loco.*

Vazquez-Arroyo, Y. A. 2019. "The Political Import of Deconstruction—Derida's Limits?: A Forum on Jacques Derida's Specters of Marx After 25 years, Part 1." *Contexto International* 41 no. 3 (Sept./Dec.): 621–642.

Wallerstein, I. 1984. *Politics of the World-Economy.* Cambridge: Cambridge University Press.

Walton, M. and S. Roy. 2012. *Globalization, Debt Relief and Poverty Reduction Concepts and Policies. Sine Loco.*

Zéphirin, Romanovski. 2017b. "Why Migrant Network and International Migration Cannot Be Schematically Separated?" Collection Immigration in the 21st Century: Political, Social and Economic Issues. In *Migrants: Public Attitudes, Challenges and Policy Implications*, edited by Stuart Rodriquez: 275–283. New York: NOVA Science Publishers.

Zéphirin, Romanovski. 2018. "The Americas' Multi-Polar Displacements as a New Pattern in Haitian-French-Guyanese Migrations." *International Migration Journal* (IOM). Available Online (01 June), https://doi.org/10.1111/imig.12470.

Zéphirin, Romanovski. 2020. *Political Demography and Urban Governance in French Guyana—Implications for Latin America and the Caribbean.* London-Singapore: Palgrave Macmillan.

Zolberg, Aristide. 1981. "Origins of the Modern World System: A Missing Link." *World Politics* 23, no. 2 (January): 253–281.

# 2

# Beyond the Evaluation of the Geopolitics and the Geo-sociology of Globalization in Latin America

## Abstract

Globalization as integrated flows in Latin America lays out various interrelated social, economic, political, and spatial networks. They challenge local-regional political systems, urban policy planning, territorial governance, transnational mobility, sociality and ethnocultural identity, social movements and sociopolitical mobilization patterns, migrants and gender rights, illegal border crossing, and urban and transnational violence and crime. While some find in market liberalization the opportunity to maximize their profits across borders, others develop anger and apathy toward free-trade zones and economic globalization through the transnational social forum as a means of promoting transnational social justice movement within globalization. As expressed in practice, the economic regionalization-globalization shows politics of scale, socioeconomic practices, social stratification, and class restructuration on transnational territories.

In consequence, the raised issues within Latin American nations point out some parameters to evaluate the significance of geopolitics and the geo-sociology of globalization. The need for some evaluative indicators requires a theoretical framework to explain the regional transformation and, more importantly, to do research on various hierarchical location, space, and place.

In this view, three theoretical armatures are combined to explain geopolitics and the geo-sociology of globalization. First, Martin and Taylor (2001) lay out the premises for a theoretical framework to manage migration and economic integration in a south-north context. Second, Donald Bogue (2003) sheds light on south-south or migrations within Latin American countries. Third, in the continuity and the rupture from the works of Massey (1987), Smith (2003), and Krissman (2005), Zéphirin (2016) connects migrant network with international migration network on a system of spaces to analyze scattered and transnational migrations within the Americas.

Finally, through the broader transnationalism paradigm evaluating economic integrative arrangements, a multidisciplinary perspective is used to highlight the complexity of migration, cities, and globalization in Latin American geopolitics.

Keywords: globalization, economic integration, migration, cities, geopolitics, geo-sociology, transnationalism, Latin America, and the Americas.

## Introduction

Import-substitution policy shift gave way to export-oriented industrial development and free-trade arrangements, causing the interaction and the interconnection of various global-regional flows and networks in the Western Hemisphere. These problematic developments beg the following question of how to evaluate the significance of market liberalization-globalization on development policy and the geopolitics in the Americas, and more importantly, beyond the empirical evaluation of the globalization-regionalization, what is its theoretical underpinning?

Free market and labor liberalization significantly affect the mobility of capital, goods, people, information, transnational territorial formation, politics of scale, and geopolitics in the Americas.

This assertion is based on literature review and some quantitative data to assess the diverse consequences of the shift in development policy as transnational migrations in network cities expressing the geopolitics of globalization.

1. *Shifting from import-substitution to export-oriented development: the regional context*

Generally speaking, cities in the Americas are marked by European colonization. Cities were put in strategic locations such as coastal areas, rivers, elevated and fortified areas, etc., to not only structure colonial territories, but also control them in terms of exclusive and sovereign rights. As a matter of fact, cities across the Americas were built with some functions and structures in order to uphold the system of production largely based on production of agricultural goods and the exploitation of some natural and environmental resources. In other words, colonial urban structures corresponded to a particular economic mode of production and a social structure, in which main colonial powers participated in, such as Spain, Portugal, Britain, France, and Netherlands.

However, with the start of rebellions and revolutions in colonies against colonizers (above mentioned), a new era of postcolonialism and independence appeared in the Americas, affecting cities. As a result, from the nineteenth to the twentieth century, new national economic, social, and political elites arose and differently changed the urban structures and their uses. Many postcolonial elites in Central (including the Caribbean) and South Americas continued to largely use the inherited colonial urban structures and their hierarchies to land and strengthen their socioeconomic, spatial, and political control of their new sovereign lands. The new independent and postcolonial dominant classes maintained, to a large extent, their commercial and cultural links with former European colonial powers. As a result, cities not only received more and diverse populations, but also, in a large measure, kept their functions of social, economic, and political dominance over rural areas and connected different parts of their countries to the external world.

However, in the path of the European, the United States in Northern America quickly accelerated the industrialization during the nineteenth and the twentieth centuries to move from a postcolonial country to an imperial one. This shift affected the cities' structures and their rural territories, their functions, their hierarchies, their demographics, and their artifacts through the modernization and the change in the forces of production. The rise of the United States as an industrial and imperial power marked the growth of its own cities that allowed new and modern economic sectors and actors to model and lead its urban settlements.

In this perspective, the United States hegemony in the region, expressed largely through the Monroe Doctrine (Manigat 1991), targeted many countries in South and Central Americas. Through military invasions and occupations, agricultural companies, and commerce, the United States' expansionism in one way or the other impacted cities and their rural territories in their agricultural production, their mode of production, and their forces of production in neighboring countries in the Americas.

The penetration of the US capitalism in many countries in the Americas changed to some degree the social, economic, and spatial structures of production of goods through economic policies and political and military influences. In some countries, the overuse of natural resources of big transnational corporations caused diverse local indigenous and national reactions to ultraliberal economic development policies and politics.

As a matter of fact, in an attempt to industrialize their countries, many governments (largely on the political left), in a perspective of reducing the political and economic dependency, decided to apply the import-substitution (Lehman 1990) as a way of national development, expressing to some degree a rejection of imperialism in the Latin American and Caribbean region. The importing-substitution approach has its own impact on cities and their rural areas. The efforts of industrialization through the creation or the reinforcement of a national bourgeoisie involved in national production for mainly constituting an internal market led some governments to nationalize some foreign companies or build new ones. All these impacted cities and their rural territories in terms of functions, use, socioeconomic structures, spatial cohesion, urban growth linked to movements of population, and rural-urban migrations.

The import-substitution model lasted from 1930 to 1980 (Stark and Jeffrey 1998, Roberts 2001), unfortunately, to a large degree, failed to achieve a high level of predicted development and economic progress for people in Latin America and the Caribbean at large. It is important to add that the presence of authoritarian regimes, brutal and corrupt dictatorships, did not help to strengthen a progressive national bourgeoisie in promoting national production and a high level of economies of scale and development.

The failure in state managing development will, in the early 1980s, presage a significant reversal in development policy approaches in Latin America and the Caribbean, of course politically influenced by the United States of America. As a result, in the early 1990s, free-market economy and free-trade economic policy will pave the way to a new era of export-oriented industrial development in replacement of the largely failed import-substitution development policy approach.

The new export-oriented economy is a corollary of globalization that started to cross and unify the countries in the Americas. According to Roberts (2001), who referred to Anthony Giddens (1990), *globalization* is defined as ''a division of labor and power.'' Irazabel (2009, 46) noted that

> Free market economics'' in Latin America was experimented in Chile under the brutal and bloody dictator Augusto Pinochet, following the advices of "Chicago's Professor Milton Friedman, called to evaluate the economy.''… The economic reforms proved successful at a macroeconomic level, but since Pinochet's human rights record was horrendous, more question the connection of free market reform, democracy and fascism.

Unfortunately, or fortunately, the successful experiment of the "free-market economics" during the presidency of the bloody dictator Pinochet has been taken by many regional and international organizations, following Professor Friedman's economic recipes to shift Latin America and the Caribbean from dictatorship to liberal democracy and economic prosperity. Once again, this is a contro-versial move fueling the claims of sociopolitical activists and social reformers against neoliberal solutions, imperialism, shrinking governments, cutting social benefits, and abandoning pro-poor policy as a way of reducing budget deficit, keeping low inflation, and promoting successful macroeconomic growth.

Aside from controversies and opposition between the political right and left on approaches of economic policies to create enough wealth to increase profits of big corporations or to redistribute economic growth and meet human needs with the context of globalization and the multiplication of integrative arrangements in the Americas, all governments, right and left, apply to some extent, "free-market economics" and free-trade policy that are inherently connected to the export-oriented industrialization and development.

In this view, the agricultural export industry, the service sector, information technologies, manufactured goods, free-trade zones, and diverse integrated infrastructures (IADB 2009) continue to grow in many countries in the Americas in the frame of export-oriented industrialization and globalization.

Once again, as in the previous approaches of economic-development policy, "free-market economics" and free-trade areas within the economic globalization-regionalization of the Americas have considerable consequences on cities and urban structures in the Americas, particularly in Latin America and the Caribbean.

2.  *Market liberalization, transnational migration, and cities in question in the Americas*

The Americas in general have been marked by European colonization. The colonial era left its imprint on rural-urban territories. In this view, not only rural areas were connected to port cities, but also, they were attributed the role to provide key natural resources and agricultural goods to both colonial cities and their European metropolitan cities.

As a matter of fact, cities in the Americas reflected the European violent penetration and dominance through their architectures, functions, location/spatial pattern, physical environment, and urban land use dynamic. Macionis and Parrillo (2009) identified some key characteristics and drivers of cities in the colonial era (1600–1800) in North America, but also to some degree the Americas at large. They (Macionis and Parrillo 2009) emphasize on colonial drivers such as "good rivers, seaports, and strategic locations."

Colonial cities are characterized by a "lack of regular street patterns and the importance of stone houses (until the eighteen century)." Colonial cities are export centers. They supplied lumbers for the ships and sending material to Europe (Macionis and Parrillo 2009).

However, it is important to relativize the idea that colonial cities were marked by "a lack of regular street patterns." On this matter, it matters to mention that effectively, if many colonial cities in some places in the Americas were drawn with an irregular street network, in other locations and, for many reasons (including economic, political, military, and physical), a regular street grid with squared urban blocks is well fabricated. Probably, the generalization of a more regular street design model that will be legalized and systematized during the industrial era had already started (to some degree) during the European colonization of the Americas.

In this perspective, the anticolonialist and the revolutionary wars that arose in the Americas, causing the independence and the constitution of new nation states that will not only push out European colonizers, but will also significantly modify (through time) the urban areas through the parameters of "administrative functions, economic characteristics, functional nature and population size and density" (Macionis and Parrillo 2009).

By the nineteenth and the twentieth centuries, the rapid industrial emergence of the United States of America as a regional power will have significant impact directly or indirectly on urban areas and their rural territories in many neighboring countries in the Americas.

That process will not go without some spatial consequences interrelated to administrative functions, economic characteristics, functional nature, and the population size.

The industrialization and the accelerated urbanization led to economic prosperity in the United States during the mid-nineteenth and the early twentieth centuries corresponding to a strong economic and military influence in the rest of the Americas. In this historical context, many parts of the Americas will be differently impacted by the US urbanization style with, among other things, high skyscrapers, large avenues, boulevards and regular street patterns, seafronts, fancy restaurants, luxury hotels, beach resorts, parks, etc., almost in the sense inspired by Daniel Burnham's neoclassical style and proposal to construct a city around monumental centers. The tendency to show the beauty of the city (city beautiful movement) marked to some extent urban planning and city development in some places in the Americas.

Example, the US influence in Cuba under the Fulgencio Batista regime (before the Castro brothers' socialist revolution) was linked to an urban plan to redesign[16] the capital city of Havana (Irazabal 2009) with casinos, luxurious hotels, and large boulevards in the seafront. Contrary to this modernization of the city devoted largely for fortunate economic actors, political elites (international and national), and also tourists from wealthy westerns countries, other rural populations in neighboring Caribbean countries were allowed to migrate to Cuba to work as cheap labor in the sugar cane industries owned by US companies.

The urban revitalization plan was assimilated by Irazabal (2009, 44) as "a US colonization and imperialism in Latin America and the Caribbean." The United States's influence on many sorts and many parts of the Americas did not totally end the European urban planning culture. Despite the US dominance in the Western Hemisphere,

---

[16] According to Irazabal (2009), the Havana urban plan under the Batista regime did not take account of the history of the city in its design and its various process of construction. In this view, a critical approach of the "architecture of the city" developed by Aldo Rossi and Peter Eissenman (2000) in urban planning reject the (simple functionalist) theoretical account, considering the city as a "white page" on which developers and urban planners can write and rewrite on and on and indefinitely without considering the historical past of the city.

Le Corbusier, a famous French urbanist, contributed to urban design and building in Brazil (Irazabal 2009).

All the above contextual elements are historical background to better problematize the interplay of economic globalization and urbanization in Latin America and the Caribbean. On this matter, the globalization, to some degree and for some segments of the urban population, sparks a certain level of informalization of the urban economy connected to individual subsistence economy and urban poverty. According to Irazabal (2009) and Roberts (2005), a poverty-reduction policy strategy linked to the promotion of tourism and service economy for global consumers causes municipal governments to remove poor people or low-income citizens from historical urban centers in order to revitalize them for a more fortunate local and international population. In this view, to some extent, globalization penetration in Latin America and the Caribbean goes in pair with a certain form of gentrification.

By the way, in terms of interacting market liberalization, transnational migration, and cities in the Americas as a contextualization of the globalization, two important aspects need to be underlined.

First, for example, in North America, Sassen (1991) noted that in the global city of New York, low-income migrant workers from some countries in the Americas benefiting from global capital investment (such as the Dominican Republic) face income and gender inequality and live in less valorized urban segments of the city. To some degree, the mobility of capital from the global financial market and the global city of New York, paradoxically, sparks important influxes of migrants from the Dominican Republic to the US (New York).

Second, in Latin America and the Caribbean, free-trade zones and labor-market liberalization linking to economic integration cause migrant workers to move across borders of neighboring countries to look for employment and better life. According to Irazabal (2009, 11),

> When migration happens across nation-states within Latin America and the Caribbean,

it is driven by an exodus of people from poorer to richer countries or from dangerous to more stable countries. Examples of these migration axes are Bolivia to Argentina, Peru and Columbia to Venezuela, Nicaragua to Costa Rica, Jamaica and Haiti to the Dominican Republic, or the Dominican Republic to Puerto-Rico. Some of the migrations happen from Latin America and the Caribbean to North America and Europe, but most particularly to the U.S of America.

In this vein, Zéphirin (2016), in a multipolar displacement of migrants creating an inter-American system of spaces where migrant networks and international migration networks are interconnected, shows that immigrants from Brazil, Suriname, Guyana, and many Caribbean countries go to the neighboring French Guyana, which represents an alternative place to failed migration attempts to South Florida shores (the US). As a matter of fact, Miami (Florida) hosts a large number of the Latin American and Caribbean population. Census from the city of Miami displays data regarding the stock of population with Latin American descent.

Table 1. Top 15 Sources of In-migrants to Miami-Dade County in 2016

| State | County | In-migrants |
|---|---|---|
| Florida | *Broward County* | 10 762 |
| Florida | *Palm* Beach County | 2293 |
| Florida | *Orange County* | 2001 |
| **New York** | ***New York County*** | 1788 |
| Florida | Hillsborough County | 1540 |
| **New York** | ***Kings County*** | 1317 |
| Florida | *Lee County* | 837 |
| Florida | *Leon County* | 787 |
| Florida | *Pinellas* County | 762 |

| State | County | In-migrants |
|---|---|---|
| **New Jersey** | *Passiac County* | 733 |
| Florida | *Alachua County* | 688 |
| Florida | *Monroe County* | 649 |
| Florida | Polk County | 640 |
| **California** | **Los Angeles County** | **610** |
| Florida | Volusia County | 602 |

(Source: 2009–2013 ACS, US Census Bureau.
Downtown Miami Demographics 2016, 11)

Table 2. Top 15 Sources of Out-migrants
to Miami-Dade County in 2016

| State | County | In-migrants |
|---|---|---|
| Florida | *Broward County* | 24200 |
| Florida | *Palm* Beach County | 3767 |
| Florida | *Orange County* | 3510 |
| Florida | *Lee County* | 1788 |
| Florida | Hillsborough County | 1469 |
| **California** | **Los Angeles County** | **1461** |
| Florida | *Collier County* | 1412 |
| Florida | *Alachua County* | 1390 |
| **Texas** | **Harris County** | **1347** |
| **Illinois** | **Cook County** | **1159** |
| Florida | *Leon County* | 1090 |
| Florida | *Duval County* | 1022 |
| Florida | St-Lucie County | 846 |
| **New York** | **New York County** | **809** |
| **Nevada** | **Clark County** | **637** |

(Source: 2009–2013 ACS, US Census Bureau.
Downtown Miami Demographics 2016, 11)

Also, a part of the population that migrated from the local state
of Florida and relocated in Miami (Miami-Dade) comes from New
York City, in the urban segment of Kings, which receives important numbers of people from the Caribbean. In other words, there

is a close connection between the mobility of migrants within the Caribbean basin moving to Florida, from New York to Miami, or from Miami to New York.

In this perspective, the local state of New York, and particularly New York City, releases data about the geographical provenance of the inhabitants. In the census, Caribbean and Latin American[17] populations are in high numbers, while the city of New York itself reflects the population of the world at large (The Newest New Yorkers 2013, 13).

The growth, the composition, the distribution, and the mobility of the immigrant population in major US cities are an important political demographic factor in terms of influencing the electoral districting and designing the local political map. The interstate mobility of the composite population in US cities often contributes to change the electoral strategies of main political parties. The demographic changes impact the political affiliation of voters and the ideological profile of local (or national) elected official leaders. In other

---

[17]

> Latin America was the top area of origin in New York City, accounting for nearly one-third of the city's immigrants. While this was a relatively large share, Latin Americans had an even larger presence among the nation's foreign-born, where they had a 47 percent share.

> Between 2000 and 2001, the foreign-born population in the city increased by 195, 600 or 7 percent from 2.87 million to 3.1 million… Dominicans were the largest foreign-born group in 2011, with 380, 200 residents or 12 percent of the total. (The Newest New Yorkers 2013, 12)

> In fourth and fifth places were two non-Hispanic Caribbean sources Jamaica (169,200) and Guyana (139,900), followed by Ecuador (137,800), and two other non-Hispanic Caribbean countries, Haiti (94,200) and Trinidad and Tobago (87,600). The foreign-born from Jamaica, Haiti and Trinidad and Tobago declined between 2000 and 2011, while the Guyanese population increased by seven percent. (The Newest New Yorkers 2013, 13)

words, population growth, composition, and spatial distribution in urban-rural areas are a crucial element of political demography and urban governance (Zéphirin 2020). The population shift from one county or one city to another not only impacts local-national politics and policy, but also, to some degree, weighs on foreign policy toward immigrants' origin countries. In this view, political demography in a context of composite population not only involves ethnosocial changes but, more importantly, political geography and geopolitics.

By the way, while globalization mainly relies on a network of investment capital, mobility of goods, and technology, the factor of labor is often neglected or is a matter of secondary importance. In this view, Orozco (2009) highlights the interest of labor and migrants for economic integration, globalization, and Western Hemisphere economic interdependence. Citing Prakash and Hart (2000), Orozco (2009, 4) identifies

> Three measures of integration of labor markets in the global economy. The first, is the proportion of foreigners in the domestic workforce. The second, is the ratio of the domestic workforce in export-dependent industries and employed by domestic affiliates of foreign MNEs'... A third measure is remittances [migration facilitates integration through remittances that contribute to a home country's GNP].

Additionally, following the definition of Giddens (1990) of *globalization* as a "division of labor and power," a particular "nation-state system, geopolitics, social, economic and military order," and the Sassen (1991) approach of networks and mobility of investment capital and fragmentation of production causing transnational migrations in global cities, it is clear that all these combined processes reflect on urban spaces and cities the consequences of the globalization. In this view, regarding Latin America and the Caribbean, Irazabal (2009, 11), referring to Sassen (1991), wrote that

> One of the most important aspects of globalization has been the provoked response of simultaneous proliferation of exclusive growth and haphazardly constructed slums. In highly urbanized metropolitan areas of which there are usually highly developed enclaves marked by global business headquarters and gated communities the rich and the poor have been separated by more than just economic lines. Latin American cities have become increasingly dichotomous in terms of wealth and class, and such divides have manifested themselves physically in contrasting urban forms... Also, in Buenos Aires [including Sao Paulo, Santiago, and Lima] alone, the number of gated communities along its northern highway more than tripled in the 1990s, reaching 500 by the year 2001...gated developments usually occupy significant areas of land and are disconnected from the regular urban street grids.

Latin American and the Caribbean countries that are involved in economic integration and the global market are facing mounting demographic pressures on their cities as urbanization rapidly grows and threatens the urban structures, their historic centers, and their traditional urban hierarchies in diverse ways.

In this view, major cities in Latin American and the Caribbean such as Mexico City, Sao Paulo, Buenos Aires, Rio de Janeiro, Lima, Bogota, Caracas, and Santiago are facing the challenge of rural-urban migration and population increase. This rapid urban growth problem goes beyond major cities to reach the midsized ones. "By 2005, what were originally metropolitan areas with hundreds of thousands in 1950 had populations of more than 5 million" (Irazabal-GRHS 2009, 8).

In the same vein, Bryan R. Roberts (2005, 117), referring to cities of Santiago (Chile), Buenos Aires (Argentina), Montevideo (Uruguay), and Mexico City (Mexico) and their struggle with urban poverty, argues that "the households most affected by poverty, as might be expected, are those in the lowest socioeconomic strata, but by the end of the decade, there is an increase in the proportions of households in the higher socioeconomic strata that experience poverty."

Also, it is important to note that the increase of the urban population linked to rural migration and affected by poverty in metropolitan areas of the abovementioned cities is an active population in the economy involving in the sectors of "manufacture, commerce, and services" (Roberts 2005, 113). Example, in terms of commerce, for the period of 1990–2000, key cities such as "Buenos Aires (16, 9% in 1990 and 17, 8% in 2000), Santiago (16, 3% in 1990 and 18, 6% in 2000) and Sao-Paulo (14, 6% in 1990 and 16, 6% in 2000)" show a slight growth in this economic sector in the data displayed by Roberts (2005, 113).

In this context of employment in commerce as one of the economic sectors, many countries in the Latin American and Caribbean region tackle the problem of informal human settlements and informal economy in their cities and particularly in historic city centers. The countries and city governments tend to push for removing informal commercial activities in cities and replacing them by more formal jobs in the economy such as revitalizing and redeveloping old historic city centers to promote tourism.

On this matter, Irazabal-GRHS (2009, 109) presented some data below by countries, quantifying the level of "informal economy as measure of productive labor."

Table 3. Informal Economy as Measure of Productive Labor in Percentage in Latin America and the Caribbean in 2007

| Selected Latin American Countries | Percent |
| --- | --- |
| Argentina | 44,10 |
| Bolivia | 76,90 |
| Brazil | 55,00 |

| | |
|---|---|
| Chile | 37,00 |
| Colombia | 71,20 |
| Costa Rica | 41,40 |
| Dom. Rep. | 51,20 |
| Ecuador | 66,40 |
| Salvador | 57,00 |
| Guatemala | 69,50 |
| Haiti | 88,90 |
| Honduras | 67,80 |
| Jamaica | 57,50 |
| Mexico | 54,10 |
| Nicaragua | 54,10 |
| Panama | 64,70 |
| Paraguay | 50,20 |
| Peru | 72,30 |
| Uruguay | 69,50 |
| Venezuela | 54,00 |
| Latin American And the Caribbean Region | 59,36 |

(Source: World Bank 2007, cited by Irazabal 2009, 109)

By the way, globalization does not limit itself to internal rural-urban migration. It also and to a considerable extent allows transnational migrations from neighboring countries. This is the case of Chile, which receives considerable stocks of immigrants from neighboring Latin American and Caribbean countries to fill some low-skilled jobs for its competitiveness in the global-regional economy.

In this category, Chile is not alone to host transnational immigrants from regional countries. Brazil, while sending migrants to the nearby French Guyana who are looking for better pay and social benefits, allows other immigrants to come from the region to work in the country.

Definitely, while some countries in the region face urban poverty and informal urban settlements, others in the frame of export-oriented industrial development and globalization successfully reduce poverty and move to the next level of fighting income and gender inequality. This is the case for example of Chile.

The poverty and inequality reduction policy strategies are largely based on empowering local communities and marginalized groups in informal urban settlements through capacity building, multisectoral participation, decentralization, and better urban territorial governance.

Chile receives immigrants from many countries in different parts of the world and particularly from neighboring ones in the Americas. In this view, according to Dona-Reveco and Levinson (2012, 6), "In 2009, the following countries are identified: Argentina (60 597 people), Peru (130, 859 people), Bolivia (24, 116 people), Equator (19, 089 people), Brazil (9,624 people), Venezuela (N/A), Colombia (12, 929 people), United States (9, 720 people)."

It is important to note that, in addition to the above populations, in the context of the Chilean military participation in the UN peace-keeping mission in Haiti in 2004 and the 2010 violent earthquake and under the request of the former Chilean president, Michelle Bachelet, thousands of Haitian immigrants travelled to Chile to work as cheap labor alongside many Latin American and Caribbean migrant workers. The steady economic growth and wealth production in Chile in the free-trade and free-market economy combined with the socioeconomic and political deterioration in some neighboring states make the country attractive for many migrants in Latin America and the Caribbean.

Aside from Chile, it is important to note that according to IOM-UN Migration (2018, 2), many Latin American countries such as Argentina, Panama, Costa Rica, Ecuador, and Canada in Ontario, Québec, Alberta, and Vancouver are crossed by intra- and extra-regional patterns of migration in the Americas.

Furthermore, while South Americans go to nearby Chile, other influxes of migrants move from south to north of the Americas and end up settling in the United States. Many South American migrants from different countries are counted in the United States. According to Zong and Batalova (2018, 3), they are mainly the following:

Colombia (783, 000 people), Peru (459, 000 people), Equator (454, 000 people), Brazil

(451, 000 people), Venezuela (351, 000 people), Guyana (269, 000 people), Argentina (181, 000 people), Chile (101, 000 people), Bolivia (72, 000 people), Uruguay (51, 000 people) and other South America (42, 000 people).

The South American migrants are concentrated in main metropolitan areas of the United States. According to Zong and Batalova (2018, 6), referring to data from the US Census Bureau, the concerned metropolitan areas are the following:

New York—Newark—New Jersey City (847, 000 people); Miami, Fort—Lauderdale—West Palm Beach, Florida (472, 000 people); Washington-Arlington-Alexandria DC (135, 000 people); Los Angeles—Long Beach—Anaheim, California (123, 000 people); Orlando—Kissimmee—Sanford, Florida (95, 000 people); Boston—Cambridge—Newton, Massachusetts (89, 000 people); Houston—The Woodlands—Sugar Land, Texas (71, 000 people); Chicago—Naperville—Elgin, Illinois (54, 000 people); Atlanta—Sandy Springs—Roswell, GA (52, 000 people); and Tampa—St. Petersburg—Clearwater, Florida (47, 000 people).

Definitely, transnational migrations in the Americas' cities linked to globalization and the search for economic opportunities and better living conditions push people in all directions in the hemisphere. These abovementioned people's movements in their diverse causes and effects produce political geographies and politics of scale, which, de facto, transcend the dichotomous locality-globality of territories and draw the contours of the geopolitics of the economic globalization-regionalization of the Americas.

3. *Economic regionalization, migration as a means of integration, and foreign policy*

Globalization penetrated Latin America in the 1990 and connected it to the global economy[18] (Pulsipher 2015). Regional economic integration has been transformed by many internal and external factors, causing important changes in migration, cities, market liberalization, and geopolitics. The significance of the transformations is considerable.

Migration, cities, and globalization sparking geopolitics as politics of scale and a geo-sociology, which result from empirically documented and evaluated free-trade zones, transnational migrations, and inclusive development issues on a scattered network of urban-rural spaces, show change in explained theoretical frameworks.

In other words, contrary to Latin American immigrations to the United States and Canada intra-Latin-American migrations linked to free-market areas, labor market liberalization, and cities, showing in some extent low-paid jobs (or fair wages in average), social marginality, social movements, sociopolitical mobilization, urban disruption and violence, human and capital mobility on an interacting transnational system of spaces can be explained by migrants' search for a better-paid job, the display of diverse socioeconomic and spatial practices in integration-reintegration on scattered network cities producing politics of scale and a geo-sociology, thus, as globalization enfolds inclusive development issues for migrants and cities.

How does Latin America fit in a free-market economy and globalization, and more importantly, what is the historical context, and what are the development policy implications?

---

[18]

> Globalization refers to global interconnected flows of money, information, goods and people transforming patterns of economic development, where local self-sufficiency gives way to global interdependence... The global economy is the worldwide system in which goods, services and labor are exchanged. (Pulsipher 2015, 31)

The end of the Cold War resulting in the collapse of the Soviet Union in 1991 has profoundly impacted the Latin American and Caribbean region. Generally speaking, import substitution development policies (Ocampo and Martin 2003) with its internal market-centered approach, personalist dictatorships, right-wing paramilitary groups, death squads, and left-wing guerrillas (Dominguez 1998, Goodwin 2001) have been largely replaced by electoral democracy, civil society enhancement, economic regionalization, and free-trade agreements (Malawer 1988, Lehman 1990). However, if the new economic and political models largely supported by the United States and the core of European Union countries (Dent 1995, Stark 1998, Paquet 2005) allowed to end politico-institutional violence (Smith and Gomez-Mera 2010), inducing forced migrations (Miller 1994, Weiner 1995), the globalization[19] of regional economies linked

---

[19] "While a global approach is premature," the region adopts a strategy of "meso-economic approach…combined with negotiation by sub-region… [and] complemented by sector-by-sector regime negotiation [or] with the development of sectoral regimes at the hemisphere level." Paquet (1999, 5) identifies six integrative structures characterize the Western Hemisphere. They are NAFTA, LAFTA/LAIA, the Central American common market (CACM), the Caribbean common market (CARICOM), the Andean community, and the common market of the southern cone (MERCOSUR).

In fact, all these economic arrangements are sub-hemispheric. They include (1) North America: Canada, the United States of America, Mexico; (2) the Caribbean: Jamaica, Trinidad and Tobago, Barbados, Dominican Republic, Haiti, Guyana, Suriname, French Guyana, Antigua and Barbuda, the Bahamas, Belize, Dominica, Grenada, Montserrat, Saint Christopher-Nieves, Saint Lucia, Saint-Vincent and the Grenadines; (3) Central America: El Salvador, Guatemala, Honduras, Costa Rica, Panama, Nicaragua; (4) Andean community: Venezuela, Colombia, Ecuador, Peru, Bolivia, Chile; (5) Mercosur: Brasil, Argentina, Paraguay, Uruguay; and (6) Cuba.

According to Paquet (1999, 2) the economic integration is conceived as means of geo-governance (i.e., territorially based governance), a process of rearrangement of the role of each sector (market-based regulation, private-public and civic partnering), and a new division of labor within the three sectors. The new integrative organizations will have to institutionally provide the basis for cooperation, harmonization, concertation, and even co-decision mechanisms, which involve the three sectors. For that purpose, mixed institutions blending these principles help countries elaborate readiness indicators, which are *price*

to democracy and democratization (Bertola and Antonio-Ocampo 2012) singles out new problems that go over the simple state-national sovereignty and its borders to encompass new lowered frontiers (Castle and Miller 2009).

The constitution of economic arrangements between countries to allow investment capital, money, goods, information, and people to freely move across borders create economic spaces and blocs (Sassen 1991, Stark 1998, Paquet 2005) on transnational territories. In this process, while the state loses some of its prerogatives to the benefits of economic liberalism and transnational capital investment, it still has to face mounting social economic pressures from the unfortunate, taking advantage from democracy and democratization to claim new rights, managing, at some point, new transnational migrant labors (Sassen 1991, 1998, 2007; Robinson 2009). Differences in market labor, wages, infrastructure, and application of integrative economic reforms to meet standards of high economic performance and prosperity divide neighboring countries between compliance to integrative (Paquet 2005, 92, 93, 95) principles and reluctance.

On the one hand, some countries show reluctance and low achievements. On the other hand, other countries point out wages' discrepancy combined with geographical proximity between countries, allowing migrant workers to look for better job opportunities. The different paces and policy approaches to get in regional economic integration process leave open the possibility to migrant workers to keep flowing across transnational borders on the short term, thus, until the economic blocs on the long term homogenize and bridge the salary gaps (Martin and Taylor 2001).

In the interval of the short- and the long-term process of the regionalized and globalized economies, old migrant networks (Massey *et al.* 1987; Krissman 2005) linked with new ones in systemic interactions and interconnections in the Americas (Smith 2001; Zéphirin 2005, 2008, 2016) through the deployment of international migra-

---

*stability, budget disciple, external debt, currency stability, market-oriented policies, reliance on trade taxes and functioning democracy.* Consequently, Paquet (1999, 2, 3, 5) concludes (as Sassen 1991) globalization is the erosion of the powers of the Westphalian nation states.

tion networks (Massey 1993, Krissman 2005) raise the issues of managing Latin America and the Caribbean bilaterally and multilaterally to avoid diplomatic tensions, conflicts, and preventive wars (Weiner 1995). Migrant influxes test the efficacy (Miller 1994, de Haas and Czaika 2013) of state border policies at a time when free trade and transnational corporations are looking for profitability through wage flexibility and cheap labor. Societies face internal migrations, indigenous population, land rights, inter-ethnic relations, transnational human trafficking, drugs, violence, and organized crimes in marginalized populations in urban centers. Latin American political systems (Dominguez 1998, Stark 1998) at national, regional, and local levels are confronting urban governance, inclusive city planning for a population with different social and cultural backgrounds, while trying to achieve both high economic performance and respecting indigenous population rights and sociodemographic diversity.

4. *Questioning market liberalization, migration, and politics of scale as geopolitics of globalization*

How do free-trade zones, transnational migrations, and inclusive development concerns become an object of geopolitics as politics of scale and a geo-sociology in Latin American globalization, or how does one evaluate the geopolitics and the geo-sociology of globalization?

The regional economic globalization paradoxically sparks (regarding national circumstances and historical periods) for some urban-rural decay, and for others economic growth, while allowing the reemergence of some disrupted spaces in the periphery. Although neighboring territories geographically close to the globalization's "central command cities" are connected to many transnationalized loci in the Americas.

Evaluative parameters of globalization are numerous and diverse. For instance, the socioeconomic, ethnic, and gender profiles of the population spatially distributed or redistributed, wages and labor conditions, standard and substandard housing, social territorial trajectories in housing mono or poly localized, transnational mobility and relations to a network loci on various geographical scales, school degrees, geo-social mobility, class formation, social stratification, social structures, and cohesion in network cities and transnational territories emerge as important (among others) indicators of the geo-sociology of globalization in the region.

Spatial distribution of people and human mobility on various transnational paces redraw the size and the composition of the population. As a result, the shift in the nature of the population and its socioeconomic expectation reflects on public discourse political attitudes toward migrants, local politics, and policy. Such a multiethnic environment with a socioeconomic diversity in living conditions pertains to social movements, working-class dynamic, sociopolitical alliances, and mobilizations. Migrants' socio-spatial and economic strategies of integration and/or reintegration diversely impact social movements and sociopolitical mobilization in cities, urban politics, and policy.

For some on the political left, they use anti-neoliberal and anti-globalization rhetoric to fuel socio-urban militancy and sociopolitical activism. To others on the political far right, foreign workers to whom urban violence and drug trafficking are often baselessly associated, anti-immigrants and xenophobic discourses are aired for political gains. In many cases, globalization and labor market liberalization are not, all the time, well accepted by the local population, while national economic policies rely on them to create growth and prosperity. In one way or the other, the contradictions of transnational mobility in capital, labor, and information technology contribute to influence politics of scale, political geographies, and geopolitics on various transnational Latin American territories.

Globalization chiefly seen as economic freedom becomes as, in some measure, universal as human rights (Ishay 2008). Paradoxically, while integrative economic policies (in the world and in Latin America) become quasi universal in western hegemonic countries and, are rightly or wrongly, associated with universal human rights, local disrupted communities and indigenous populations by claiming territorialized ethnocultural rights as a means of resisting to globalization penetration put at stake in some measure the universal dimension of human rights by particular traditional cultural rights claims in Latin America and the Caribbean.

Additionally, migrants who are allowed by transnational corporations and national states' pro-integrative economic policies create a double standard in salary regime for economic profitability and competitiveness as the globalized economy is fragmented, decentralized, and interconnected (Sassen 1991, Robinson 2009).

Once again, universal human rights do not fully benefit all working-class and labor migrants as human beings in terms of respecting the dignity, equality, and security principles (Ishay 2008). Thus, while local and national legislation put first the economic rights of transnational corporations and firms in free-tax zones, low-skilled workers, immigrants, and particularly undocumented young women don't have equal human rights (regarding equal work for equal pay) across enlarged transnational borders (Sassen 1991).

As a result, to paraphrase Ishay (2008), to some extent, transnational migrations show some controversies in indiscriminately applying universal human rights in an age of global migrations (Zolberg and Benda 2001, Castle and Miller 2009). Probably, interstate managing of transnational migration crisis (Weiner 1995) as a dimension of globalization, at least for those who practice it with their feet (Goldin 2001), as border crossers and migrant workers offers a path for better compacts and multilateral cooperation (Barghava 2006) to overcome double standard in applying nationally universal human rights principles for all across transnational borders.

The post-Cold War era in the Americas and increasing globalization put forth transnational migrations, controlling borders to tighten entry to undocumented migrants, transnational crimes, and violence in an age of new technologies of information and communication. Some of the ill effects of economic globalization spark human rights and cultural rights issues in indigenous populations on enlarged and multiscale territories with reduced state authority in favor of big private corporations (Saskia 1991, Robinson 2008). Further, transnational people movements linked to globalization raise the controversial issue of the role of the statal power, which is often torn between defending and protecting human rights (Ishay

2008) and preserving safety and security or balancing both through democratic institutions as a means of meeting universal human rights requirements to indiscriminately promote broader human development.

In this view, economic globalization and migration in the Americas point out historical controversies in universal human rights, which paradoxically open new problematic grounds to increase and strengthen human rights, aside from declarations, agreements, and legislations to a continuous fight to fully (not specific categories of rights) universalize and materialize human rights for all human beings (in the Western Hemisphere), having not only basic rights and basic needs to satisfy, but also multidimensional and indivisible rights in order to meet broader human needs (Barghava 2006) and development. This perspective extends and associates the concept of human rights with security policy and not against the legitimate rights of citizens and immigrants.

The interrelated economic, social, political, and spatial (among others) issues trace the problematic contours of migration, cities, and globalization in Latin American geopolitics (Barton 1998, Denoon 2017). In this view, Latin American globalization and its integrative arrangements that induce transnational immigrations in international regional network cities (Sassen 1991) show, among other things, a considerable voluntary amount of return migrations (Zéphirin 2008, 2017), driving scattered transnationality on disrupted local communities and territories.

The analysis of the interconnected factors above lays some concrete problematic bases to move to some key conceptual definitions. Geopolitics[20] (Dominguez 1989) is conceptualized through

---

[20] Regarding the former Cold War geopolitics in interstate relations, which focuses more on bilateral diplomacy and security, there is a clear shift with the contemporary or new (in the post-Cold War) geopolitics as a matter of geoeconomics in the globalization in the Americas. This theoretical framework matters to better contextualize and analyze facts related to security, peace, and democracy in the Americas. In this view, while the work of Dominguez displays a high academic expertise, some aspects of his analysis lack to put in a broader theoretical context overlapping the political and security factors with the

predominant geoeconomic dimension of the globalization to capture the true meaning and the whole picture of some security, peace, and democracy in the Western Hemisphere. For example, in few words, the analysis of Dominguez (1989) can be summarized by some key words to qualify the post-Cold War in Latin America and the Caribbean, which are "crime pandemic, military and guerrilla demobilization, state security forces depletion, gangs and other non-state violence, drug trafficking, civil and military relationship, democratic constitutional government, security dilemma, security cooperation etc."

As stated previously, they are accurate. However, while they refer to the post-Cold War, the analysis gave to some degree the impression that the weight of the theoretical mindset is still there (partially). A clearer shift would be made, for example, of the facts of "military demobilization" "better cooperation between countries such as Brazil, Argentina…for peace" if they could be integrated in the broader framework of the political economy theory of the globalization, which is also part of the new political geography and critical geopolitics of the Americas.

"Moreover, Argentina, Brazil and Chile well exemplify dimensions of the classic security dilemma, but their interstate relations perhaps have never been better as we see below" (Dominguez 1989, 7).

In other words, the overlapping of peace security within the geopolitics of the globalization would give a larger theoretical political geography framework to interconnect and seize the crucial questions of the predominance of geoeconomics over the old geopolitics of security and understand the role of the liberal political economy theory through economic integration to promote peace and prosperity among nations. Such a critical geopolitics lens, which includes the theoretical dimension of the political economy theory in international relations, would allow to explain the role of the common economic interests through market liberalization and common economic policy as an element of coordination, of rationalizing the reduction of the high number of soldiers among main countries that do better (than others in the South Cone) in economic growth and prosperity (Brazil, Argentina, Chile).

The work of Gilpin (1997) and Malawer (1999) on the "political economy theory and international relations advocates for a win-win" policy in trade agreement to promote peace and prosperity and curb tensions and war among the nations involved in the globalization. On this matter, the liberal complex interdependence within the global economy intends to achieve peace through cooperation and integrative bodies to curb tension and war among nations, contrary to a classical realism in international relations (Keohane and Nye 1987), which is overtly conflictual. Also, the predominance of the geoeconomic rationale of the globalization in the post-Cold War era would give a significant insight to understand the "security dilemma" and the "civil-military relation"

practical issues and daily life activities on the ground. The search for better-paid jobs across national borders and within nations in the Americas adopting market liberalization economic policy creates a change in the composition of the population with different socio-economic, cultural, and ethnic backgrounds. The spatially redistributed and ethnically recomposed populations torn by different logics of integration (immigrants) and/or reintegration (return migrants) diversely impact cities and their urban neighborhoods.

In an environment of sociodemographic changes in cities and urban neighborhoods, sociopolitical mobilization impacts local politics and local policy. Added to the local-national sociopolitical movements and institutional representation and management of the sociodemographic and spatial changes, interstate cooperation, in an attempt to control at some point transnational people movements, stands out in transnational contemporary issues. The interrelated factors connecting local-national and regional urban-scale prob-

---

and the "stability of the constitutional democratic government" in the region of the Americas.

In this view, the work of Mercille (2008) regarding political geography, critical geopolitics, and radical geopolitics within the globalization offers an interesting problematic path to follow in the analysis of the cooperation, the tension, and the dominance of the geoeconomic logic of the globalization over the traditional "prerogatives," "behaviors," and influences of some military establishments in many countries of the Americas at a time of the liberal economic regionalization-globalization. To some degree, a problematical reorganization of the rich information presented and analyzed by Dominguez (1998) would be better off if it could be integrated into a specific theoretical lens or a comparative theoretical perspective. This theoretical guidance would make some deductions more consistent, more pertinent, and more coherent with the problematization of the facts involved in the analysis of "peace, security, and democracy" in Latin America and the Caribbean in a context of both post-Cold War interstate relations and liberal interdependent regional-global economy (Agnew 2003, 2005; Agnew and Corbridge 1989; Keohane and Nye 1987). These remarks matter to blend the facts and explain them into the broader existing scientific literature on the matter (thus, despite the high quality of Dominguez [1989] work). Consequently, this is one of the reasons why, in this book, the geoeconomic primacy as a matter of contemporary geopolitics of the post-Cold War era is prioritized.

lems caused by the globalization of regional economies are drivers of politics of scale, political geographies, and geopolitics. Free market and labor market liberalization, in their causes and effects in Latin America, go over a simple traditional lens of geopolitics, narrowly defined as political and military spheres of influence. Politics of scale is an attempt to politically and institutionally cope with socio-urban problems and the diversity of the socioeconomic background of a recomposed and transnationalized population redistributed on various interconnected geographical spaces.

The perspective of interconnected networks of people on diverse geographical scales develops various social interactions and interrelations with social life and forms of sociality affecting social structures in both origin, third, and host countries of immigrants, migrants, and return migrants.

Diverse socioeconomic and sociopolitical networks of actors and practices on transnational and interconnected network loci, under the circumstances of integrated regional economies, break the traditional conceptual meaning of space and place to give way to a geo-sociology generated by globalization.

5. *The theoretical implications of the interconnections of global-regional flows and networks*

The geopolitics, the politics of scale, and geo-sociology become inherent to globalization that are expressed through migration and cities in Latin America raise a threefold issue in terms of development policy shift, practical evaluative consequences, and explaining theoretical framework.

Beyond the empirical evaluation of free-trade areas and labor-market liberalization, what is the theoretical underpinning of geopolitics, politics of scale, and geo-sociology? And more importantly, how is doing research and testing hypotheses on transnational migrations and globalized network cities in the Americas?

Adhering to interrelated factors and combined internal and external determinants in studying migrations, does not stop the useful empirical observations and facts to come up and reveal both autonomous individuals' and groups' strategies in taking advantage of their migration projects, which are consubstantially and interactively associated with origin, third, and host countries' initiatives, knowledge, and know-how. These elements have methodological implications and require (among other perspectives) to also study migration by itself, while taking account of its diverse interconnected causes and effects and, more importantly, in its (migration) double dimensions, immigration, and return migrations as a means of understanding globalization, cities, territorial formation, community disruption, spatial reemergence, and connection to global transnational geographical scales.

Diverse theoretical accounts contribute to highlight the problem of global-regional flows and networks. However, in order to unify and integrate complementary theories, The argumentation uses the paradigm of transnationalism[21] (Sassen 1991, Robinson 2009), which involves capital investment mobility, internationalization of production, labor migrations, network cities, and anti-neoliberal social movements[22] (Langman and Morris 2001, Hamel et al. 2001, McKane 2014) in the globalization process. Theoretically,

---

[21]

> Transnational relations refer to cross-border relations that did not involve national states as key actors: multinational corporations, tourism, international non-governmental organizations, religious associations and so forth. The growing importance of trans-frontier migrations as an instance of such transnational relations [raises problematic attentions of academics].
>
> Transnational relations [studies] during 1970s and 1980s are distinct from international relations. (Robinson 2009, 7)

[22] Fueled by local identity problems at microscale, network sociopolitical mobilizations for democratic political change in the "public sphere" at mesoscale and trans-border network social movements at macroscale fight ideologically neoliberalism and globalization to endow social forum worldwide and promote the global justice movement.

the transnationalism paradigm[23] (Barghava 2006) transcends and intertwines some key immigration and return migration factors, interconnecting transnational labor migration, work market liberalization, cities transformation, interethnic relations, rural-urban disruption or reemergence, social structure recomposition, socio-urban movements, sociopolitical mobilizations, and politics of scale as geopolitics.

In this view, the complexity and the diversity of human logics in transnational displacements, labor, and living on many loci cause to theoretically connect migrant network (Massey 1987, Sassen 1991, Weiner and Teitelbaum 2000) and its economic, social, and political dimensions to international migration networks (Krissman 2005, Zéphirin 2005, Zéphirin 2017a) as a system of spaces (Smith 2001; Zéphirin 2016, 2017b) interconnected one to another at the geographical scale of the Western Hemisphere. This key theoretical approach intertwining migrant networks and international migration networks is keen to address migration and cities in Latin America in an age of globalization (Castle and Miller 2008).

In consequence, this main theoretical corpus of migrant network and international migrant network on a system of spaces refers to other complementary theoretical accounts.

---

[23] For his part, Bhargava (2006), in an effort to precise other dimensions in the concept of transnationalism portrayed as regional-global affairs, briefly underlines four pillars to delimit it. First, it crosses national boundaries and affects people transnationally. Second, each issue directly and indirectly in all countries of the world is evidenced by a UN (United Nations) declaration or a global conference. Third, each issue goes over a simple power of a national government or a market-based solution and requires a global regulatory approach. Four, each issue is interconnected and needs a multidisciplinary approach and consensus. Further, for Barghava (2006, 410), a transnational and global-regional issue shows not only interaction and interconnection, but is also a pressing development problem calling for action on a multilateral level. As a result, the author identifies five thematic building blocks linking to transnational regional-global issues, which are the following: the global economy, human development, environmental and natural resources and sustainability, regional-global peace, and security and global governance.

In an economic theoretical standpoint, Martin and Taylor (2001), addressing globalization, free trade zones, and migration, show that salary discrepancy on the short term creates an increase in migration flows, and only on the long term with the closing of the salary gap will the net migration decrease significantly.

Also, Miller (1994), Weiner (1995), Weiner and Teitelbaum (2000), and Bueker (2005) emphasize on theoretical public international law, political and geopolitical dimensions of international migrations, and security impacts in terms of supranational and multilateral diplomatic bodies to use coercive force against sending countries or to manage unwanted and forced migrants.

Additionally, while theoretically, Massey (1987) points out the appealing of external job creation poles to migrants in order to constitute their network in host cities, Sassen (1991) focuses on the urban social network and its effects on social structures in "central command cities" of globalization. In other words, in its causes and effects, human transnational mobility on scattered loci sparks a social geography of territories (Di Meo 1998), allowing neighboring countries and their network cities to interconnect to one another as a system. As a result, urban growth or cities are not only a simple network, but also a network of territories (Dupuis 1998). Regional transnational people movements and human settlement patterns are driven by the mobility of capital investment and migrants' strategies of integration and/or reintegration, revealing the complexity for interethnic relations in private-public housing, urban neighborhoods, inclusive urban policy, and local territorial governance. Migration influxes settled on network territories, while in their early stages, they are largely based on economic factors. However, return migrations seem to show a more complex process in decision-making, involving a more autonomous approach.

Furthermore, De Gourcy (2005) and Ma Mung (2008) point out the autonomous and voluntary human decision-making process in migration as an attempt to be free from economic overdetermination of the migration event.

In contrast, in a theoretical standpoint, Zéphirin (2016), while partly supporting the autonomous account only in reversible migration (Domenach and Picouet 1995) or in an internal one, largely opposes to it as an explicative account of international migration. Contrary to De Gourcy (2005) and Ma Mung (2009), Zéphirin (2016, 2018) conceptualizes the autonomous perspective as a return transnational migration issue and not as an international migration one.

As a result, Zephirin (2016, 2018) emphasizes on geo-social and political transnationality linked to a migrant network (or in plural) and international migration network, producing a regional system of spaces for migrations.

In this perspective, Barton's (2003) works on the political geography of Latin America, go over traditional approaches of border, territorial disputes, and military alliances to shift his research focus on daily and various human practices in different geographical scales as a means of political geography consequential of interrelated social, economic, and political processes linked to globalization, democratization, and other crucial transnational issues in Latin America.

By the way, in explaining the theoretical gap between south-north and south-south migrations, Donald Bogue's (2012) researches reveal that south-south migrants don't have the same social and financial leverage than those moving south-north on the American continent. These theoretical findings are important to highlight the complexity of south-north and south-south migrations, paradoxically interconnected in globalization and its various networks on the overall region.

In this view, the increasing in capital investment mobility in the region which penetrates local communities linking *micro, meso,* and *macro* geographical scales, causes not only social apathy and anger and sociopolitical mobilization against the free trade areas, but also paves the way to explore transnationalism through global social movements (Hamel et al. 2001, Langman and Morris 2001, McKane 2014) in reaction to globalization.

The abovementioned complex problematic elements stand out a multidisciplinary contribution completing the theoretical armature, allowing to explain and evaluate whether the geo-sociology and the geopolitics of Latin American globalization work to the advantage or the disadvantage of migrants. Thus, in an environment where the global liberalization of goods and capital markets has proceeded at a much faster pace than the international liberalization of regional labor markets, which has been liberalized internally at the national level by legislating away many of the protections labor formerly enjoyed under the prior international system of investment ISI regimes. In other words, the significance of transnational capital investment, production, labor market liberalization, and human mobility in network cities or urban-rural areas generates interrogations on prior knowledge production, research methods, and theoretical approaches. Questioning the context of research production allows to recalibrate analytical tools and redefining conceptual instruments and their cycle in terms of construction, deconstruction, and reconstruction. This is a real epistemological concern to solve in a perspective of doing research and testing hypotheses on fluctuating populations moving on multiscale and borderless territories.

Aside from general epistemic concerns specifically, how do both the practical evaluation and the chosen theoretical explaining frameworks fit in studying people movements and human settlements on scattered loci?

Market and labor liberalization through free-export zones, fragmentation, and decentralization of production show a diversity of actors involved in the regional globalization. However, different individuals, groups of people, and social classes interacting in the economic regionalization unevenly benefit from it. As a result, the Americas' globalization has its discontents (Stiglitz 2002). In this view, sociopolitical mobilization theories and political practices in free-trade countries stand out as a reaction of discontent (for some) to economic liberalization and globalization in many neighboring countries. The social marginality, poverty, and forms of collective action and social movements in free-trade areas affect the transnational workforce. That entire dynamic differently impacts migration, cities, globalization, and politics of scale in the Americas' geopolitics.

Violence-inducing forced migration correlates with urban crime as transnational issues. In an attempt to maintain civil peace and state order in borderlands affected by transnational gang violence and other traffics, neighboring states create bilateral channels to address human insecurity problems in various spaces. These transnational issues requiring state-to-state relations and cooperation appear as politics of scale and geopolitics in the Americas at large. They directly or indirectly impact migration, cities, and globalization.

The traditional approaches used in urban reconstruction plan are questioned in regard to the diversity of actors and interests practiced in Latin American cities. They are dominantly influenced by prominent economic sectors or big corporations in their design, function, and management. These actors are more interested in building the city very largely based on a patronal urbanism, rather than putting urban and territorial planning both as a quest for a political middle ground among various actors practicing the local-regional and transnational territories in the perspective of globalization. In an urbanistic standpoint, it becomes important to spatially redefine urban politics and policy planning as a means of socioeconomic and political inclusion of a diversity of actors with competing interests on scales of transnational and globalized territories in Latin American geopolitics.

## Conclusion

Finally, the multiplicity of transnational actors involved in the movement of people, money, goods, services, and information across Latin America reduces at some point the dominant role of sovereign states to alone tighten or design border policies. Globalization sets the various conditions of world-regional politics. Complex actors and interests evolving around the economic regionalization compete, negotiate, and cooperate in order to take advantage in market liberalization. The international political economy (Gilpin 1987, Sassen 1991) and the economic integrative arrangements (Paquet 2005) in Latin America spark their regional international institutions and regimes (Keohane and Martin 1995) to manage the complex interdependence (liberal approach of international politics of globalization) of state and nonstate actors (Zolberg 1981a, 1981b; Miller and Papademetrious 1983; Keohane and Nye 1985; Keohane and Martin, 1995) linking states, markets, and societies.

The rise of market liberalization and economic integration considerably scales down the state-to-state relationship classical realist approach in international relations (Keohane and Nye 1985) based primarily on military capability and conflicts (Keohane and Nye 1987) to scale up the role of innovation technology, fragmentation of production, export-capital, and wealth creation of private actors and big transnational corporation. Considerably, these elements shape and determine the international politics of migration through states' entry and exit rules (Weiner 1985, Mitchell 1989).

States and big corporations compromise over controlling borders. Globalization, by intersecting state and nonstate actors, not only reconsiders traditional priorities in terms of "high" and "low" politics in international relations, but more importantly, becomes a subject matter of increasing importance in world-regional foreign policy. As a matter of fact, globalization appears (to some extent) as a factor of reducing or solving conflicts and fostering cooperation among nations (Snidal 1991, Genest 1999) and transnational actors in order to achieve peace, prosperity, and stability.

In spite of the interdependent connection of regional economies creating room for cooperation and mutual gain, some states, while benefiting from the market and labor liberalization, still continue to see migration, forced migrations, and refugees as a security threat and are willing to take preventive military action to deter refugee flows or unwanted immigrants.

Immigration weighs on some states' behavior in their struggle for more influence and power or to balance power (Morgenthau 1987) as a matter of relative or absolute gains (Powell 1991, Snidal 1991) in Latin American geopolitics. While globalization and its interdependent complex (Zolberg 1981a) actors significantly impact regional interstate relations through the cooperation on global-regional flows, it downplays (without eliminating it) the military capability role and the prospect of war in a game of balance of power in interstate relations. However, some states, which often marginalized themselves on this matter, still refer to the military option in foreign relations as a pretext of a national security issue to prevent "anarchy" and state instability or regional insecurity in neighboring countries.

Definitely, consequential to market and labor liberalization, transnational labor migration, forced migration, and refugee instrumentation in state behavior become an object of geopolitical influence through states' political gains in regional politics and balance of power.

Now, putting this in perspective, the subject raises the issue of comparing the different geographical scales and some countries in the Americas to see the territorial formation processes and their governance as political geographies and geopolitics.

# References


Barton, Jonathan R. 2003. *A Political Geography of Latin America* (eBook). London: Taylor and Francis.

Bertola, Luis and Jose Antonio Ocampo. 2012. *The Economic Development of Latin America Since Independence*. Oxford: Oxford University Press.

Bhargava, Vinay. 2006. "Introduction to Global Issues." In *Global Issues for Global Citizens. An Introduction to Key Development Challenges*. Edited by. Vinay Bhargava: 1–28. Washington, DC: World Bank.

Bogue, Donald J. 2012. *The Economic Adjustment of Immigrants to Twelve Nations of Latin American and Comparison with United States*. Population Research Center and Center on Aging. Chicago: The University of Chicago.

Bueker, Catherine Simpson. 2005. "Political Incorporation Among Immigrants from Ten Areas of Origin: The Persistence of Source Country Effects." *International Migration Review IMR* 39, no.1 (Spring): 103–140.

Castle, Stephen and Mark J. Miller. 2009. *The Age of Migration: International Population Movements in the Modern World*. New York: Palgrave Macmillan.

Czaika, Mathias, and Haas de Hein. 2013. "On the Effectiveness of Immigration Policies," in *Population and Development Review:* 487–508.

De Gourcy Constance. 2005. *L'autonomie dans la migration. Réflexion autour d'une énigme*. Paris: L'harmattan (Collection Logiques sociales).

Denoon, David B. H. 2017. *China, the United States and the Future of Latin America*. New York: NYU Press.

Dent, W. David. 1995. *US-Latin American Policy-Making. A Reference Handbook*. Washington, DC: Library of Congress.

Di Meo, Guy. 1998. *Géographie sociale et territoire*. Paris: Nathan Université.

Domenach, Hervé and Michel Picouet. 1995. *Les Migrations*. Paris: Que Sais-Je? PUF.

Dominguez, Jorge I. 1998. "Security, Peace and Democracy in Latin America and the Caribbean. Challenges for the Post-Cold War Era." In *International Security and Democracy—Latin America and the Caribbean in the Post-Cold War Era: 3–28.* Pittsburgh: University of Pittsburgh Press.

Dupuis, Gabriel. 1991. *L'urbanisme des réseaux—Théories et méthodes.* Paris: Armand Colin.

Genest, Marc A. 1999. *Conflict and Cooperation: Evolving Theories of International Relations.* Belmont, CA: Thomson and Wadsworth.

Giddens, Anthony. 1990. *The Consequences of Modernity.* Stanford University Press. Stanford, CA.

Gilpin, Robert. 1987. *The Political Economy of International Relations.* Princeton, NJ: Princeton University Press.

Goldin, Ian. 2006. "Globalizing with Their Feet: The Opportunities and Costs of International Migration." In *Global Issues for Global Citizens. An Introduction to Key Development Challenges.* Edited by Vinay Bhargava: 105–121. Washington, DC: World Bank.

Goodwin, Jeff. 2001. *No Other Way Out: States and Revolutionary Movement, 1945–1991.* New York: NYU Press.

Hamel, Pierre, Henri Lustiger-Thaler, Jan Nederveen Pieterse, and Sasha Roseneil. 2001. *Globalization and Social Movements.* New York: Palgrave MacMillan.

Irazabal Clara, 2009. *Revisiting Urban Planning in Latin America and the Caribbean.* Columbia University, New York. Available from http//www.unhabitat.org/grhs/2009.

Ishay, Micheline. 2008. The *History of Human Rights: From Ancient Times to the Globalization Era.* Los Angeles, California: The University of California.

Keohane, Robert O. and Joseph S. Nye. 1987. "Power and Interdependence Revisited," *International Organization,* 41:725–753.

Keohane, O. Robert and L. Lisa Martin 1995. "The Promise of Institutionalist Theory." *International Security,* 20 (1):39–51.

Krissman, Fred. 2005. "Sin Coyote Ni Patron: Why the Migrant Network Fails to Explain International Migration." *International Migration Review (IMR)* 39, no.1 (Spring): 4–44.

Langman, Langman and Douglas Morris. 2001. *Internet Mediation: A Theory of Alternative Globalization Movements.* https://www.scribd.com/doc/316333582/Morris-Internet-Mediation.

Lehman, David.1990. *Democracy and Development in Latin America. Economics, Politics, and Religion in the Post-War Period.* Philadelphia: Temple University Press.

Macionis, John J. and Vincent N. Parrillo. 2009. *Cities and Urban Life* (5th ed.). Pearson: New Jersey.

Malawer, Stuart S. 1988. "The Political Economy of International Relations by Robert Gilpin." In *Maryland Journal of International Law* 12, no. 2, article 6: 307–311.

Ma Mung, Emmanuel. 2009. "Le point de vue de l'autonomie dans l'étude des migrations internationales: penser de l'intérieur les phénomènes de mobilité." In Françoise Dureau; Marie-Antoinette Hily, *Les mondes de la mobilité*: 25–38. Rennes: Presses de l'Université de Rennes.

Martin, Philip L. and J. Taylor Edward. 2001. "Managing Migration: The Role of Economic Policies":95–120. In Aristide Zolberg and Peter M. Benda, *Global Migrants Global Refugees. Problems and Solutions.* New York: Berghahn Books.

Massey, Douglas S. et al. 1987. *Return to Aztlan: The Social Process of International Migration from Western Mexico.* Berkeley: University of California.

Massey, Douglas. 1993. "Theories of International Migration," *Population and Development Review,* 19 (3).

McKane, Rachel. 2014. *The Globalization of Social Movements: Exploring the Transnational Paradigm Through Collection Action Against Neoliberalism from Latin America to the Occupy movement.* In Pursuit—The Journal of Undergraduate Research at the University of Tennessee, vol. 5, issue 1, article 11. http://www.tracetennessewe.edu/pursuit/vol5/iss1/11.

Miller, J. Mark. 1994. "Introducing the Critical Transparency School of Immigration Analysis." In Wayne A. Cornélius, Philip L.

Martin., and James F. Hollifield (eds.). *Controlling Immigration. A Global Perspective:* 107–112. California: Stanford University Press.

Miller, Mark J. and Demetrios G. Papademetriou. 1983. "Immigration and U.S Foreign Policy." *In the Unavoidable Issue: US Immigration Policy in the 1980.* Edited by D. G. Papademetriou and M. J. Miller. Philadelphia: Institute for the Study of Human Issues.

Mitchell, Christopher. 1989. "International Migration, International Relations and Foreign Policy." *IMR-International Migration Review,* volume xxiii, no. 3:681–708.

Morgenthau, Hans J. 1978. *Politics Among Nations: The Struggle for Power and Peace.* New York: Alfred A. Knopf.

Ocampo, Jose Antonio and Juan Martin. 2003. *Globalization and Development. A Latin American and Caribbean Perspective.* Santiago, Chile: ECLAC.

Orozco Manuel, 2009. ''Globalization and Migration: The Impact of Family Remittances in Latin America''. *Journal of Latin American Politics and Society.* Volume 44/ Issue 2. Summer 2002. Published online by Cambridge University Press: 02 January 2018: pp. 41-66.

Paquet, Gilles. 1999. *On Hemispheric Governance (PDF Download Available)* https://www.researchgate.net/publication/228393060_On_Hemispheric_Governance (accessed on March 26, 2018).

Paquet, Gilles. 2005. *The New Geo-Governance. A Baroque Approach.* Ottawa: University of Ottawa Press.

Powell, Robert. 1991. "Absolute and Relative Gains in International Relations Theory." *American Political Science Review* 85, no. 4: 1303–1320.

Pulsipher, Lydia Mihelic and Pulsipher Alex. 2015. *World Regional Geography Concepts* (Third Edition). New York: W. H. Freeman and Company, Macmillan Education Company.

Roberts R. Bryan, 2005. ''Globalization and Latin American Cities''. *International Journal of Urban and Regional Research.* Volume 291. 10-25 pp. March.

Robinson, William I. 2009. "Sassen Saskia and The Sociology of Globalization. A Critical Appraisal." In *Sociological Analysis* 3, no.1 (Spring): 5–30.

Sassen, Saskia. 1991. *The Global City: New York, London, Tokyo.* Princeton: Princeton University Press.

Sassen, Saskia. 1998. *The Mobility of Capital and Labor: A Study in International Investment and Labor Flow.* Cambridge: Cambridge University Press.

Sassen, Saskia. 2007. *A Sociology of Globalization.* New York: W. W. Norton.

Smith, C. William and Lora Gomez-Mera. 2010. *Market, State and Society in Contemporary Latin America.* New York: Willey Blackwell.

Smith, C. Robert. 2001. "Current Dilemmas and Future Prospects of the Inter-American Migration System," in A. R. Zolberg and P. M. Benda (Ed.), *Global Migrants Global Refugees—Problems and solutions*: 121–167. New York: Berghahn Books.

Snidal, Duncan. 1991. "Relative Gains and the Pattern of International Cooperation." *American Political Science Review,* 85 (3):701–726.

Stark, Jeffrey. 1998. "Globalization and Democracy in Latin America." In *Fault Lines of Democracy in Post-Transition Latin America*: 67–96. Edited by Felipe Aguero and Jeffrey Stark. Miami: North-South Center Press at the University of Miami.

Stiglitz, Joseph S. 2002. *Globalization and Its Discontents.* New York and London: W. W. Norton and Company.

Weiner, Myron. 1995. *The Global Migration Crisis. Challenge to States and to Human Rights.* New York: Harper Collins.

Weiner, Myron and Michael S. Teitelbaum. 2001. *Political Demography—Demographic Engineering.* New York: Berghahn Books.

Zéphirin, Romanovski. 2005. *Le Champ migratoire haïtiano-guyanais: étude des causes et effets politiques, socio-économiques et spatiaux. Multipolarité et réversibilité dans le système migratoire interaméricain.* Aix-en-Provence: Thèse de Doctorat sous la direction de Hervé Domenach, Université Aix-Marseille III, Faculté de

Droit, d'Economie et des Sciences-IUAR (Institut d'Urbanisme et d'Aménagement Régional).

Zéphirin, Romanovski. 2008. "L'émigration-rémigration des Haïtiens dans l'espace interaméricain comme fin du modèle sociétal du pays en dehors—Repenser le développement," *Revue Migrations-Société* 20, no. 117–118, mai-août: 11–24.

Zéphirin, Romanovski. 2016. *Les réseaux de migrants haïtiano-guyanais dans l'espace américain*. Paris: L'Harmattan.

Zéphirin, Romanovski. 2017a. "The Politics and Policy Implications of Widespread Immigrations in French Guyana." In *Migrants: Public Attitudes, Challenges and Policy Implications*, edited by Stuart Rodriquez: 59–110. New York: Nova Science Publishers. Collection Immigration in the 21st Century: Political, Social and Economic Issues.

Zéphirin, Romanovski. 2017b. "Why Migrant Network and International Migration Cannot Be Schematically Separated?" In *Migrants: Public Attitudes, Challenges and Policy Implications*, edited by Stuart Rodriquez: 275–283. New York: NOVA Science Publishers. Collection Immigration in the 21st Century: Political, Social and Economic Issues.

Zéphirin, Romanovski. 2018. "The Americas' Multi-Polar Displacements as a New Pattern in Haitian-French-Guyanese Migrations." *International Migration Journal* (*IOM*). Available online (01 June), https://doi.org/10.1111/imig. 12470.

Zéphirin, Romanovski. 2020. *Political Demography and Urban Governance in French Guyana. Implications for Latin America and the Caribbean*. London-Singapore: Palgrave Macmillan.

Zolberg, Aristide. 1981a. "International Migrations in Political Perspective." In *Global Trends in Migration: Theory and Research in International Population Movements*, edited by M. M. Kritz, C. B. Keely, and S. M. Tomasi. New York: Center for Migration Studies.

Zolberg, Aristide. 1981b. "Origins of the Modern World System: A Missing Link." *World Politics* 23, no. 2 (January): 253–281.

# 3

# The Mobility of Capital, Labor, and Human Beings in Residences between Haiti and French Guyana in Questioning Transnational Migration and Territoriality as Political Geographies

## Abstract

Workers follow the capital. The regular transfer of capital from the core metropolitan France to the overseas department of French Guyana in the early 1970s was to support local public budget and building infrastructural development. The need for a larger and cheaper labor force sparked many immigrants to move to French Guyana. All neighboring Caribbean countries are involved, including Haiti. Haitian immigrants built a community there. And through time, autonomous urban integration and reintegration processes between French Guyana and Haiti have changed migrants' rationales and practices. A part of migrant workers and job seekers become entrepreneurs and employers in their host society. They are engaged in remittances. And in many cases, money transfer is used for diverse purposes, including building private houses.

On this matter, choices of voluntary integration or reintegration within the immigrant community considerably impact the frequency, the amount, and the periodicity of remitting, saving and investment patterns on both sides of the migration stream. Also, human and residential mobilities are conditioned by the decision to definitely settle in the host country or to move back to the home society. In their diverse causes and effects and in the long term, autonomous Integration and reintegration choices of immigrants reverberate on land use and change in terms of spatial production through the extension of the stock of built private houses both in the origin and receiving country. Through the construction of new houses and the back-and-forth on both sides of the migration stream, particularly in the practices and the changing social and spatial trajectories, migrants create new territories reflecting their new perception of periodically living in new dwellings in both countries.

This dynamic of voluntary human settlements and the resettlements spark new social practices in houses across borders and, more importantly, political geographies by creating new and dispersal territories, causing public policy concerns. The practice and the migrants' perception of their new lands and homeownerships make sense of a new territoriality in living and circulating on scattered loci going over the simple geographical scale of French Guyana and Haiti to encompass the whole Western Hemisphere. In the wake of shifting immigration policy from attractive to repulsive, uncontrolled border crossers cause bilateral and multilateral cooperation and geopolitical issues as an attempt to curb unwanted influxes of migrants.

Consequently, in the long term, binational migrants' networks with their shifting practices in labor, capital, human beings, and residential mobility show a geo-sociology of transnationality that transcends the theoretical gap between migrant networks and international migration networks. And in the Americas' broader context of regionalized globalized economy with its transnational migrations in transnational urban network systems, definitively the transnational territoriality and its reversible migrations become a new and complementary dimension in the research object of the sociology of globalization.

Keywords: labor, capital, migrant, mobility, transnational territory, territoriality, political geographies, Haiti, French Guyana, the Americas, and globalization.

# Introduction

Migrants' transnational territoriality sparks political geographies.

How do different labor, capital, human, and residential mobility factors impact long-term migrants' choices of voluntary urban integration-reintegration, causing a transnational territoriality between Haiti and French Guyana?

In an attempt to shed light on this interrogation, the chapter asserts that an external pool of employments in French Guyana attracted numerous Haitian temporary guest workers who rapidly constituted a community; however, in the long term, immigrants themselves in their individual, collective, and autonomous choices toward their sending and receiving countries deploy new financial practices, housing constructions, and socio-spatial networks, pointing out transnational territoriality and political geographies.

This chapter that uses different sources of data and research findings (Zéphirin[24] 2005, 2016) to support its assertion aims at showing that from short term to long term, labor, financial, people, and residential mobility go over the dual "push-pull factors" to reach an interrelated "cause-effect" relationship regarding the evolution of the migration project as consequential of both voluntary integration-reintegration decisions of immigrants and the formation of transnational territories.

1. *Private-public investments, migrants' status, and transnational remittances*

At the beginning of the 1970s, the French state decided to financially help the overseas departments to fill the development gap that separates them with the core metropolitan France departments and regions (Zéphirin 2005). As a result, under the principle of national solidarity policy reinforced through the decentralization

---

[24] I am very grateful to two sought-after experts and emeritus professors, namely Mark J. Miller in the US and Hervé Domenach in France, who kindly and respectively wrote the foreword and the preface of my first book published in 2016.

of the territorial management during the 1980s, the core France regularly transfers public funds to support many public activities relative to local budget and governance. The external public funding from metropolitan France to its local administrations was mainly oriented to finance: social policy, public servants, infrastructures, public buildings, roads, etc.

The transfers were legitimated by the fact that the local wealth production and the fiscal dish were too tiny to uphold by themselves the increase in financial spending that the new status of department (French Guyana move from the status of overseas territory to overseas department) required. For instance, in the 1980s, more than 266 million French francs (Castor and Othily 1984, 134) have been transferred to French Guyana as public funding to support the administrative budget and the public running of local state institutions in the department. In this perspective, public transfers continued to grow in millions of francs[25] (Castor and Othily 1984, 134).

The regular transfers allow an important circulation of money, which has considerable incidences on the economy of the department in terms of accelerating importation of some goods fabricated in the core France, urbanization and housing construction, and positive impact on the GDP. While the growth could be seen in some regard as an artificial one, however, it contributes to boosting the employment in many economic sectors, particularly in public buildings and private home constructions. As a result, in 1974, the combined public and private constructions rank this economic sector number one in job creation in French Guyana, attracting 70.4 percent of the active population in the local job market (Chantilly 1980). The attraction of the construction also affected an important part of the traditional rural agricultural workforce who shifted from seasonal agricultural jobs to more steady employments in construction. This mutation in the workforce that reflects on low- and mid-skilled workers' socioeconomic and professional profiles corresponds well with the context

---

[25] The French national currency before the adoption of the Euro. The francs have been spent for the following years of 1976 (326.4 million), 1977 (314 million), 1978 (364.9 million), 1979 (370.4 million), and 1980 (563.4 million).

of immigrant waves that came from many nearby countries in the Caribbean basin, including Haiti.

In this perspective, many of the Haitian rural poor peasants and low-skilled workers found in French Guyana a pool of new job opportunities and a possibility for a better living. This is the reason why the pioneers started moving from Haiti to French Guyana. Despite the fact that they came in principle in a program of "temporary guest worker," for many internal and external reasons (Zéphirin 2016), they became definitive immigrants in the long term. Now, they are part of the French Guyanese demography and society. In other words, the short-term displacement of the "base residence," its main activities and individuals' life from Haiti to French Guyana, is now transformed in a long-term project, sparking a change in the nature of the mobility, which became a migration event (Domenach and Picouet 1995).

Two key elements relate to the constitution of the Haitian immigration in French Guyana.

First, in the middle of the 1960s, a French investor called Lucien Ganot involved in an agro-industry plant in southern Haiti decided to partly outsource some segments of his production from Haiti to French Guyana. As a result, he brought with him a contingent of fifty immigrants[26] as pioneers (Gallibourg 1995, 25) to set up his farming business.

---

[26] Mainly, in the early 1970s, Haitians began to enter in French Guyana. The first group was composed of fifty immigrants (Gallibourg 1995, 25). Additionally, in Guyana, in 1982, Haitian migrants presented this gender profile: 62.8 percent of males and 37.2 percent of females. However, the Haitian feminine immigration distribution shifted from 27 percent to 39 percent between 1974 and 1985, and of these, women ranging in age groups between twenty to twenty-five years old represented 13 percent in female migrants, with twenty-five to thirty-five years old forming 51 percent of the general Haitian population (Chalifoux 1988, 79). This statement of Chalifoux is consistent with data published by the French Census Bureau in Guyana (INSEE-Guyane 2003). According to these data, the Haitian female population (7,450) has augmented to the detriment of the male one (6,693). Also, in general, Haitian migrants reported a population growth of 285 in 1968 to 48 in 1969 and 50 in the 1970s (Piantoni 2002, 371).

Second, in the early 1970s, the French government in core metropolitan France launched in the overseas department of French Guyana[27] a significant initiative to invest in an infrastructural development initiative and an agricultural project (Chalifoux 1988, 79) as well.

Both private and public investments were combined to attract (INSEE-TER 2000) a considerable number of Haitian immigrants in French Guyana.[28] When these pools of job opportunities were opened, Haiti had an increased unemployed[29] rural population (Girault 1975; Zéphirin 2005, 150). In order to reduce the probability for social tensions and unrests, political instability, and insti-

---

In 2004, it increased at a phenomenal rate, reaching 14,143 people (INSEE-Guyane-TER 2003, 45).

[27] Moreover, the decentralization initiated by the Act of 2 March 1982 (concerning the rights and freedom of municipalities, departments, and regions) and (followed by) the Decree of 1st July 1992 giving priority to consultation between the *Prefet* (local representation of the French national government) and local elected representatives have paved the way to a mutation in the status of Guyana. Local politicians took advantage of this context of decentralization and deconcentration to claim, expand, and reinforce new social, political, and economic rights in Guyana. "The improvement of the means of action of the local authorities presupposes a questioning of the current legal framework" (Rubio 2000, 48). In this view, while N. Rubio (2000) mainly referred to the French Caribbean overseas departments, French Guyana did not differ from them.

[28] Haiti: Population (7,000,492), fertility rate (4.8 percent), life expectancy M/F (48/52), HDI rank (159), GDP/Resident in US dollars (413) US dollars (817), exports in millions of US dollars (241) (INSEE-Guyane-TER, Caribbean indicators 2000, 9).

Note that in 2017, the total population of Haiti is estimated at ten million inhabitants for a total of 27,500 square kilometers.

French Guiana: Population (157,000), fertility rate (3.5), life expectancy M/F (73/79), HDI rank (33), GDP / Resident: (10 480), importation in millions of dollars US (536), exports in millions of US dollars (116) (INSEE-Guyane-TER, Caribbean indicators 2000, 9).

Note that in 2017, the total population of French Guyana is estimated at 281,314 inhabitants for the total areas of 90,000 square kilometers.

[29] 86 percent (forty-three interviewees out of fifty) of the Haitian immigrants declared to be motivated by employments when they migrated to French Guyana in the early 1970s.

tutional destabilization caused by the fast-growing socioeconomic disparities, the personalist oppressive dictatorship of Duvalier (the son, called baby doc) allowed numerous Haitians—mainly the rural poor—to immigrate to French Guyana, where they could find the employment[30] and the wage they could not get in their home country. Doing so, the national government of Haiti released the sociopolitical and socioeconomical pressures on his own shoulders. Sending migrants to the neighboring French Guyana allowed private agro-industrial plants to benefit from cheap labor and to maximize their annual profit. Also, the French state took advantage of the low- and mid-skilled workers by reducing at some point the cost of salaries in infrastructural development[31] projects. Consequently, both sides

---

[30] At the beginning of the decade of the 1970s, Haiti, with a total population of 5,095 (in million) outclassed Dominican Republic (4,200) (in million) and Guatemala (5,034) (in million). Additionally, Haiti, in comparison to the Dominican Republic and Guatemala, presented a higher density and a higher number of population depending on agricultural jobs to get a living. For example, while Haiti has a density (inhabitants/km2) of 180, the Dominican Republic and Guatemala respectively differ with 83 and 45 inhabitants on square kilometer. Also, in terms of percentage of agricultural employments in the GDP, once again Haiti takes the lead with 47.9 percent, followed successively by Dominican Republic (24.8 percent) and Guatemala (27.3 percent).

[31] The seventh plan, commonly called the Green Plan or, in French speaking, Le Plan-Vert, proposed by Olivier Stirn, had set precise objectives. Between 1976 and 1978, on the population having obtained subsidized financing:

- 18 percent are migrants, accounting for 32 percent of the financial envelop
- 57 percent are "persons settled in Guyana," with 21 percent of the allocation
- 51 percent of them have sought or have been able to obtain loans of less than 30,000 francs

The Green Plan, in addition to its concerns to change the traditional agricultural system of Guyana, also set out to exploit the physical environment more rationally and to use the potential of the foreign population for the benefit of the agricultural economy. Agriculture received grants and loans of CHF 122 million. In addition to infrastructure work, over five years, this credit increased in 1979 from 43 million to 122 million (Castor and Othilly 1984, 174). Note that the French Franc currency was in use prior to the Euro currency (adopted in January 2000 in France), which has an exchange rate of approximately six French francs for one Euro.

of the Haitian-French Guyanese migration stream benefited (fair or not) from the immigrants.

From the decades of the 1980s and 1990s, the Haitian migration in French Guyana[32] was associated with some specific economic sectors of employment.

A large part of the Haitian population is regrouping in Cayenne (Piantoni 2002) in search of paid employment in the intermediate sector. It is a population largely made up of low-income workers who represented the bottom of the social hierarchy in interaction with the system of production of goods and wealth.

In terms of socio-professional and occupational profile, the immigrants are largely mechanics, scrap dealers, housekeepers, masons, foremen, etc.—workers who are unemployed, and looking for job opportunities reach a large number (Zéphirin 2016) with the completion of major infrastructural development projects in the mid-1980s.

This context favored ethnic migrant entrepreneurship and the creation of micro enterprises in the Haitian community in Cayenne in the mid-1990s. The Haitian immigration, which has always been perceived as a burden by right-wing local politicians and in public office in French Guyana (Zéphirin 2017a), or as an opportunity by various private employers, gradually differs from these two visions of public attitudes toward immigrants. Haitian immigrants, after a little more than five decades of wealth accumulation through small business creation, participate (at some point) in the production of added value in their host society. The small group of Haitian entrepreneurs intervenes at a certain level in the economic circuit. They contribute

---

[32] Countries that send immigrants in French Guyana (INSEE 2000, 9) include Surinam (17,654 or 37.9 percent), Haiti (14,143 or 30.4 percent), Brazil (7,171 or 15.4 percent), Guyana (2,372 or 5.1 percent), European Union (846 or 1.8 percent), Dominican Republic (673 or 1.4 percent), countries in the Americas (582 or 1.2 percent), Saint-Lucia (525 or 1.1 percent), Indian Ocean Islands (38 or 0.1 percent), and other countries (2,572 or 5.5 percent). In all, foreigners in French Guyana totalize 46,576 people (INSEE-Guyane, TER 2003, 45). These countries are the main contributors to the population growth in French Guyana in the past decades.

to transactions and through their activities by which they renewed both employees-staffers and fresh capital and investments (Zéphirin 2016).

As a result, the simplistic view that states that the Haitian migration is a "burden" for the host society needs to be significantly downplayed. The new pool of "immigrant investors" (Bernstein and Weiner 1999) not only creates jobs for the community, but also crosses ethnic lines to employ people with different national origins. In other words, the economic development of the Haitian immigrant community through ethnic business (Zéphirin 2017) in French Guyana relativizes in some measure the social investment burden weighted on the public finances of the state, at least for the stock of the first generation of immigrants.

The growing number of the Haitian immigrant population, employment in agricultural farms, in road infrastructures, the construction of the space center of Kourou (Chantilly 1980, Castor and Othilly 1984) for launching satellite capsules, and small business owners contribute to flow money in the immigrant community. However, a part of the money circulating[33] in the Haitian-French

---

[33] A survey has been organized on both sides of the Haitian-French Guyanese migration stream, which totalized one hundred questionnaires separated in two groups of fifty for French Guyana and fifty for Haiti. We added and combined economic variables (remittances, plane ticket fees, and investment) with a survey of questionnaires (fifty) in Guyana on the data of ninety-five marriages registered at the town hall in Cayenne-Guyana and with a file of 6,020 passports delivered by the Haitian consulate to the citizens of this country who migrated to French Guyana.

The file of 6,020 passports helped me (Zéphirin 2005) to both realize qualitative interviews with a focus group (120 people) to deepen the survey on both sides of the migration stream. I have been done that to well measure on both sides of the migration system variables and their indicators like provenance (milieu), demographic (male/female rates and age-squared), socio-spatial (zones of provenance in Haiti), the neighborhood of residence in Cayenne-Guyana, mobility of residence, and socio-professional category. In the frame of a descriptive statistic method (percentage, medium), a transversal approach (analysis of the moment on a particular period of time) and not longitudinal (life history) has been adopted to treat the data and comparing it with the results of my quantitative pooling.

Guyanese[34] (Zéphirin 2012, 2016) migrant network (Massey et al. 1987, Krissman 2005) will be oriented toward the origin country. Largely, the immigrants send money[35] (Zéphirin 2014, 430) at

---

By the way, the survey has been balanced on both sides of the Haitian-Guyanese migration stream. To do so, two transnational variables have been elaborated: "sending/receiving money" and "spatial trajectories in residence" in the two countries both separately and interactively.

In others, the space variable is defined in French Guyana from three loci (Eau-Lisette, Bonhomme, and Balata). These sites express dynamics of the first settlements of immigrants and their mobilities in residences in the Cayenne agglomeration.

The total area covered by the observation is about twenty-five kilometers long along the road, connecting the three communes of the Cayenne's agglomeration. The survey has been randomly administrated on the sites. It is vital to realize the survey at the same scale and to balance it on both sides.

At the reverse, in Haiti, a complementary survey took place also. It selected two sites: one before the emigration and a second, a new one, built mainly by return migrants. If the observation has been done on a scale of twenty-five kilometers long along the national road number 2 from Miragoane, Fond-des-Nègres to Aquin, the main pools by questionnaires selected the nucleus village of Fond-des-Nègres to survey people both on the right side and on the left side of the ancient and the new national road number 2 crossing the village.

Habitats in the old site of the village express an obsolete social way of life before the emigration, however. New houses raise up on both sides of the new road point out a kind of transnational manner of life in new architectural types. Integration/reintegration processes in both societies engender a great socioeconomic mobility of people on various spaces across borders. To measure the transnational hierarchy of territory effects of integration/reintegration, some specific variables concerning neighborhood of living and urban trajectory not only in French Guyana, but also in Haiti before the emigration and after the remigration have been adopted in close correlation with remitting behaviors.

[34] The great majority of people in Fond-des-Nègres migrates to French Guyana at 85 percent (or thirty-five cases) and only 9.8 percent (or four cases) in Florida (the United States).

[35] Migrants who dream of someday moving back to Haiti transfer amounts of money exceeding four hundred US dollars. This amount represents more than 17.1 percent (or seven cases) of the total migrants involved in making such transfers. Solely, 2.4 percent (or one case out of forty) wired one thousand dollars.

In terms of remittances from French Guyana and their reception in Haiti (in Fond-des Nègres, southwest of Haiti), 53.7 percent (or twenty-two cases)

home to family members on a regular basis to support fundamental expenses and the rising of the cost of living. Migrants' remittances[36] (Marcelli and Lowell 2005) from French Guyana are mainly transferred on a monthly basis (Zéphirin 2012) to pay for high schools, food, buy plots of land, and build houses. If remittances[37] (Zéphirin 2016) are mainly directed to relatives or the inner circle of a family, also other extended family members or close friends could also occasionally receive money transfer from migrants.

Additionally, while a segment of the immigrant community decides to regularly send money to the origin country for many purposes (already mentioned above), other groups in the immigrant community differ in their trends concerning remittances[38] (Zéphirin

---

have received remittances in 2001 ranging from US $100 to US $200. About 24.4 percent (or ten cases) of recipients have had from two hundred to three hundred dollars.

[36] Marcelli and Lowell (2005, 77) citing Massey et al. (1987) posited and wrote that "We conceptualize remitting as a decision made by individual migrants who are oriented toward both home and host community."

[37] To better understand the various logics of the number of the population transferring money and the amounts transferred by the migrants, it is necessary to correlate them to the frequencies of sending. That data expresses in some ways the kinds of choices of integration or/and reintegration on both sides of the migration stream. Remittances and their frequencies are often trimonthly (72 percent or eighteen cases) than monthly (8 percent or two cases) or yearly (8 percent or two cases).

[38] According to Zéphirin (2017) citing IADB (2007, 13), the United States represents 71 percent of remittances and French Guyana only 1 percent. If this data is only considered at a macro level, it generally reflects the reality of remittances. However, if it is refined through a critical analysis involving various source countries of emigration, then the limitations for understanding all the complexity of emigrations, links, and scales of territories that connect host and origin countries will become more evident. For example, my (Zéphirin 2005) own observations and inquiries in the southeastern subregion encompassing Miragoane, Fond-des-Nègres, and Aquin (particularly in Fond-des-Nègres) show that people primarily migrate in French Guyana at 85 percent and then receive their money from there, when only 9.8 percent of recipients get it from the US (Florida). The data (Zéphirin 2016, 152) regarding the Haitian migrant network in Fond-des-Nègres and its scattering aspects stands out clearly. So if IADB (2007, 13), in a preoccupation to segment remittances by regions in Haiti, presented different percentages for south (55 percent), the center (62

2012, 38; 2014, 427). Instead of regularly transferring money, they mainly invest it in their home country in priority where they buy plots of land, build new houses, and open a small or midsized business in their new homeland. They send money to the home country on an irregular basis to some people being identified as part of their extended family and not (only) to their inner family circles, who often are already reunified with them or are about to do so.

Consequently, for some, the urban neighborhood locations, the housing conditions (standard or substandard), the choice of transferring money, and its amount and its frequency depend by and large on their willingness either to definitely settle and fully integrate the host society or for others, to prepare in the long term the total reintegration in the origin country (Zéphirin 2008, Zéphirin and Piantoni 2009). Accordingly, housing construction, land purchasing patterns, and urban relocation practices reverberate on voluntary integration-reintegration decisions between French Guyana and Haiti.

2. *Urban relocation and land practices as migrants' integration and/or reintegration*

At the commencement of the migrant network in French Guyana, immigrants settled in self-segregated urban areas where they could share the same national and even rural local values in their new urban neighborhoods. However, in the long term, after a certain period of time where money accumulation started to grow and family members began to reunify on one side or the other of the migration stream, the immigrants entered a new phase in their spatial occupation patterns. They partly started moving from their initial and historical urban areas, often poorly equipped and substandard, to a more standard and well public-serviced neighborhood or newly built urban infrastructures. Particularly, those on their way to integration[39]

----

percent), north (5 percent), the southeast (29 percent), Artibonite (33 percent), and Grand-Anse/Nippes (36 percent) it did not problematize these different regions in regard to the multipolarity of displacements and the host countries.

[39] "Integration goes beyond a simple question of origin or territorial belonging of people to encompass the society as a whole. It refers to the common good and

(Costa-Lascoux 1999, 101; 332) in their host society, opt to break urban community barriers and to peacefully coexist with other ethnic groups (Touraine 1997) in the society.

Often, this socio-urban attitude is supported by changing personal and financial conditions of immigrants who show the willingness to partly invest their accumulated money to transform their way of living in a socially more valued and a more decent urban area. Also, the integration of immigrants is favored by national and local state authorities who promote intercultural relations in urban housing and as a means of fighting exclusion and poverty (Chuhan 2006).

In French Guyana, particularly in the Cayenne agglomeration (Zéphirin and Piantoni 2009), before moving to their new urban quarters, immigrants used to live in precarious conditions. They are often considered as unfortunates who live in substandard housing and ill-serviced urban neighborhoods. Thus, because most of the homes were previously abandoned by their owners in downtown Cayenne, their former proprietors moved to suburban single family houses or mansions on the communal territory of Remire-Mont-Jolly. Inhabitants, largely composed of undocumented immigrants and documented low-income working-class immigrants, don't have the proper income to pay for standard housing on the real-estate free market. They are mainly renters of their dwellings, which are most of the time equipped with risky power grid connection or simply without electricity, without piped water, absence of sanitary or pick-up trash system, and being overcrowded.

Immigrants' settlements on the basis of national origin or geographical provenance from the home country become a factor of not only building trust within the urban ethnic community but also an arrangement to share both the cost of daily living and the monthly fees of the rent to the landlords, who sometimes exaggerate the bill in order to take advantage of immigrants' "fragile" conditions.

In the long term, financial accumulation and savings over the years combined with the decision to voluntarily integrate into the host society have motivated urban relocation from the downtown of

---

the integrity of people and their rights to fulfil their citizenship."

the Cayenne city to other neighboring communes of the agglomeration. Urban mobility became the best way to escape housing's precarious conditions in which numerous immigrants lived for so long. As a result, residential mobility of a segment of the Haitian immigrant population collides with land practices, changes in the legal status in land property, and housing ownership. By and large, many new single private family homes relocated on newly built urban areas were previously situated in shanty towns or in densely populated urban neighborhoods in the central city of Cayenne (Zéphirin 2005).

The Haitian population spatially redistributed partly coincides with newly built houses with backyards. The immigrants who choose to integrate buy plots of land and construct big houses in newly recomposed urban areas with mixed populations. This new socio-urban and intercultural dynamic in new urban fragments in Cayenne's nearby communes spark urban planning and local territorial governance issues. And as the state is technically well equipped and financially rich enough to deal with the spatial recomposition underway, it promotes urban and social inclusion while supporting new infrastructure development projects. However, at the micro level, the redistribution of the population generates profound local political changes in some urban areas in communal territories such as Matoury and Cayenne.

For instance, the redeployment of the Haitian immigrant population, largely naturalized French citizens, weighs on the local electorate and the outcomes of urban sectoral elections (Zéphirin 2005, Bueker 2005, Zéphirin 2016) in Matoury. In its political causes and effects, the residential relocation translated into spatial redistribution significantly contributes at some point to redraw the urban political map (Zéphirin and Piantoni 2009). The inter and intraurban migrations in the Cayenne agglomeration create new political geographies in terms of setting up a network of spaces with different human and political rationales both for the new French citizens with migrant descent and for local politics and politicos.

Housing shortages and sociopolitical pressures to satisfy the public need in standard homes raise home availability as a public problem requiring a public policy response from the local political system (Zéphirin 2017a). In this context, urban planning and local urban governance become a way to provide coherence to the peripheral urban territory in turbulence (Brunet 1990), caused by a lack of standard housing constructions, unplanned urban infrastructure, and residential mobility at different scales of the Cayenne agglomeration.

This is the broad socio-urban and infrastructural context in which the tendency for voluntary integration emerges and affects the urban relocation of a segment of the Haitian immigrant community. As a result, immigrants who opt to return to their Haitian homeland of origin also impact the spaces of both the host and the origin country in different manners. The pro reintegration[40] currently first chooses to live in Cayenne's shantytowns with the purpose to set aside enough money and move back home, where often many immigrants start to build their "dream houses" for which they have migrated more than three decades ago. Constructing new big private houses becomes, in their view, a matter of successful reintegration, socioeconomic self-fulfillment, and social prestige in front of their countrymen staying at home.

Additionally, in the rural source country of emigration now facing voluntary return migrations, the newly built houses create de facto urbanization in the rural village of Fond-des-Nègres (Southern

---

[40] Haitian immigrants who live in the Cayenne agglomeration in shanty neighborhoods of Eau-Lisette and Suzini (Boutezelle) and Bonhomme opting for reintegration (return migration) are more likely to transfer money in Haiti on a regular basis. They remit money to family members in Haiti most of the time in intervals of three months (i.e., 72 percent, or eighteen cases out of twenty-five surveyed inhabitants in the abovementioned urban area of Eau-Lisette). It has shown that inner urban neighborhoods in Cayenne invest more money in Haiti than in French Guyana.

It is also important to mention that similar to the findings in Eau-Lisette and Bonhomme, people from precarious urban zones in Cayenne-Guyana are more involved in remittances.

The Haitian pole of the migratory stream and the project of return migration from French Guyana play a key role in Haitian remittances. Thus, in Haiti, about 51 percent (or twenty-one cases) of Haitian return migrants in the nucleus village of Fond-des-Nègres were mainly from French Guyana, 4.9 percent (or two cases) came from Canada, and 2.4 percent (one case) from Florida / the United States of America (Zéphirin 2005, 254).

Haiti). The village is spatially reconfigured as a consequence of the growth of newly built houses, differentiating the old spatialized archetypes in the traditional rural village with the newly built areas. The rapid augmentation of new dwellings correlated to return migrations caused the central national government to decree and grant the status of commune to Fond-des-Nègres, which by the way shifts from a communal section to a full status of commune. As a result, the redeployment of return migrants combined with internal (inter and intra) nearby migrations plays an important role in both scaling up the rural population and enlarging the built surface of the town, the hotbed of the community emigration (Domenach and Picouet 1995, Zéphirin 2005) to French Guyana.

In terms of construction practices, returning migrants or would-be ones (living in French Guyana) buy pots of land alongside the national road number 2 crossing the center of the commune of Fond-des-Nègres. My observation field (Zéphirin 2005) pushed me to focus on the process of changing trajectories in the host city of Cayenne as a means of socio-spatial integration[41] and/or reintegration at both individual and collective levels. The spatial strategy to get rid of social exclusion in the city consists of moving from one poorly serviced urban neighborhood to another decent one in the broader Cayenne agglomeration.

Often, urban settlement and residential mobility both relate to the rationales of integration in the French Guyanese host society and/ or the Haitian origin country. In this view, the result of my inquiry (Zéphirin 2005) shows immigrants who are involved in residential mobility lived long ago long ago in abandoned houses in downtown

---

[41]   Data on "access to constructible land by invading" (44 percent or eleven cases), "payment through a plan policy to a public notary" (40 percent or ten cases), or "payment to the legal owner" (8 percent or two cases) shows that people who choose to voluntarily integrate themselves in new urban neighborhoods in Matoury in the Cayenne agglomeration have a very slight financial margin in regard to conditions of access to land or to financial efforts to legalize the status of the occupied land. So even if they cannot easily (or don't) transfer the money to their native country, they nonetheless make some important investments in their host country, French Guyana (Zéphirin 2005, 352).

Cayenne or other well-known slums (as Eau-Lisette, Bonhomme, Suzini etc.) in the city's outskirts. The socio-spatial integration logic drives the immigrants to move to the nearby city of Matoury, which has a larger urban land reserve. In consequence, Haitian immigrants are relocated in newly built urban areas in Matoury (Balata, Cotonnière, and so on). They expressed a clear tendency for voluntary socio-spatial integration in decent private family houses. Before buying a plot of land in Matoury, moving, and owning their private homes, Haitian urban residents lived in a precarious condition in housing with a status that can be labeled as guests, tenants, and cotenants or subtenants. Generally speaking, occupants rent from a landlord in the abovementioned urban areas.

Also, the urban relocation of Haitian immigrants in the Cayenne agglomeration collides with some particular land use and practices that are in some regard complementary to the socio-spatial integration process where different tactics were used, such as squatting of land, negotiating payments by installment with the legal owners to legally buy the land invaded, and the connection of the newly built land and neighborhoods to the urban grid (Zéphirin 2009, 2016).

In this view, putting in coherence disparate actors' strategies (Friedberg 1997) in managing the urban growth and sprawl caused by the individual production of urban segments, the in city, through a complex negotiation with diverse actors with different rationales, goes over a simple technical approach in urban management to encompass a broad strategy. The implementation of a socio-technique approach includes urban technical advisors architects, geometers, engineers, urbanists and urban planners, social reformers, urban activists, and local civil society organizations. The diversity of actors practicing and producing the city with different interests is the reason why to set the stage and institutionalize sociopolitical dialogue in order to find a common ground as a means of participatory urban planning and inclusive public policy efficiency (Zéphirin 2017).

The participatory approach based on partnering and networking in the local urban policy in a context of immigrants' integration allows easing intercultural and interethnic relations in the urban public space in order to avoid a confrontational strategy that could push further in exclusion of the already marginalized poor in the city.

3.  *Human mobility both in housing and across borders as transnational territoriality*

Human mobility problematized as transnational territoriality[42] brings, up front, three different levels of territories[43] (Di Meo 1998, 39, 41) and practices in correlation to Haitian-French Guyanese immigrants' biographies. First, human mobility in housing as socio-spatial trajectory in both immigrants' sending and receiving countries is linked to integration-reintegration. Second, border-crossing and border-region practices as a means of transnational territorial formation between origin and host countries relate to repulsive immigration policy.[44] Third, inter-American multipolar people movements through the origin, transit, and destination countries as

---

[42] "From the 1970s to 2004, 10 people made the trip Haiti-Guyana in 3 times, 3 people in 10 times, 6 people in 4 times. Over 30 years of immigration 4 percent of travelers admit to have returned more than 20 times in Haiti" (Zéphirin 2016, 112).

"Passenger traffic according to destination and origin at Rochambeau Cayenne airport for the year 1999 [points out] Port-au-Prince: arrivals 2,292, departures 2,515 and total 4,807" (Piantoni 2002, 405).

[43] "Territory groups and associates loci and makes a collective sense of them, and more importantly goes beyond their concrete practice… Territory is a general organization of loci reflecting their true social meaning and arrangements."

[44] "72 percent of Haitian immigrants in Guyana compared with 28 percent at the airport entered to the territory by the Surinamese border. Many irregular Haitian migrants travel between Haiti and Guyana without French visas or residence permits in France. They go through neighboring Suriname and go to Haiti without any problem" (Zéphirin 2005, 127).

transnational[45] (Robinson 2009, 7) territoriality[46] (Di Meo 1998, 39, 46) connected to migrants' strategies and new routes undermine the policy of prohibiting illegal border crossers.

Additionally, human mobility in housing sparks transnationality in loci between French Guyana and Haiti. The residential mobility on the Haitian side of the migration stream undergoes significant changes on the composition, the carrying capacity of houses, and their sociality. In the southwest part of Haiti, particularly in communal rural areas such as Fond-des-Nègres, La Colline, and Marseillan, located between the midsized cities of Miragoane and Aquin, the stock of newly built houses grows considerably.

For instance, the increase in private constructions caused the former Haitian prime minister Gerard Latortue to decree Fond-des-Nègres as a commune in 2004. The locality moved from a territorial status (Brunet 1990) of communal section in rural areas to a full commune itself. According to Zéphirin (2016), in the old rural nucleus village of Fond-des-Nègres, the human density was high, approximately five or seven inhabitants in private family dwellings. However, in the newly built sector, not only are houses bigger, but also the human density is lower and periodically varies between three and five people (Zéphirin 2005). The reduction in the number of occupants of the homes occurs because the owners live abroad, and few very close family members show a human presence as a means of occupancy of the property. The presence of occupants who are from the inner circle of the owners provides at some point some dissuasive

---

[45]

> The study of transnational (as distinct from international) relations emergent cross-border relations that did not involve national states as key actors: multinational corporations, tourism, international non-governmental organizations, religious associations, and so forth... Sassen Saskia insisted on the growing importance of cross-border migrations as an instance of such transnational relations.

[46] "Territoriality is a desire of territory, a material and an immaterial exchange between humans and their territory... Territoriality refers to the linkages and behaviors toward the territory."

security against acts of theft and sabotage. The true owners often go back and forth between Haiti and French Guyana periodically and use the newly built houses as a pied-à-terre.

This is the reason why the houses largely correspond with an unstable and transnational human population living in a semiretirement situation. Most of the homeowners spend half of the year in both countries. Also, the size of the house matches with the willingness of return migrants to socialize with the extended family or the new generation of the family born abroad and in Haiti. In other words, the kinds of sociality within the new dwellings allow, in some degree, to unify different parts of the family scattered on diverse loci in the inter-American space. Thus, until the migrants return back definitely, of course, if certain key security measures or other infrastructural conditions are met in the origin country.

That is not so sure to have all the requirements met in Haiti. Probably, the dream of a definitive return to Haiti under some unfavorable circumstances could spark an endless migration to other countries, or to French Guyana again or to other more peaceful and safer places in the Americas, where some old migrants with their money could find peace and good life. That could be their last resort if the general situation of the country does not allow them to fully return home and fulfill their dream of reversible migrations.

However, if in Haiti the returning process that is underway meets some security issues and other challenges related to the general condition of the country, in French Guyana, the conditions are more favorable to those who choose to mainly stay there definitely. Thus, they continue to maintain at some point some unbreakable links with the origin country.

Changes in Haitian immigrants' houses in French Guyana depend on the aspirations of socioeconomic promotion. In a socioeconomic standpoint, residential relocation ensures a closer proximity to the workplace. It reduces the commuting distance between home and work in the city. For the Haitian immigrants, each change in a neighborhood corresponds to a new socio-financial situation that is transmuted on the dwellings. Even in precariousness, there is an effort toward comfort, which symbolizes a manifestation of social success. The urban mobility of the immigrants in the agglomeration of Cayenne interacts with new neighborhoods (Zéphirin and Piantoni 2009) in a network of spaces. The newly built town houses in Matoury accommodate reunified families and, in some degree, express a sense of a new sociality. Often, when the part of the family stayed at home after decades of immigration decides to emigrate, the head of the household has to prepare the material conditions to make it happen.

One of them is the dwelling for the family, which has to be decent and spacious enough to welcome the newcomers. As a result, the newly built houses are places that socially differ from the old and crowded homes that settled the pioneers when they first came. The new habitations purposively receive the inner circle of the head of the household or simply his or her nucleus family. Consequently, the human mobility in urban residences coincides with not only a social trajectory in houses, but more importantly, establishes a particular relationship with the space and the place.

As a matter of fact, the interaction of human activities on space through physical construction and the perception of people of their own life at some point in their biographies reorder the territory and, more importantly, make new sense of it in terms of territoriality by projecting their own newly redefining identity on the territory.

Definitely, through a problematization of human mobility, residential relocation, and social practices in urban housing, it appears a translation of different phases of emigration, immigration, and migrant and return migration on human life that reverberates on space as territoriality largely modeled by the voluntary integration-reintegration choices between the old homeland and the new home country.

Furthermore, border crossing[47] (Zéphirin 2016) and border region of transnational territorial practices between the Haitian ori-

---

[47] Taking account of the primary research, data produced by quantitative questionnaires (Zéphirin 2005, 179) on the interactions among neighboring countries with French Guyana in terms of immigration shows along with the rationale that more than 72 percent (or thirty-six cases out of fifty) of the Haitian population emigrated and crossed the borders of these countries

gin and the host French Guyanese societies relate to repulsive immigration policy.

The adoption of a repulsive immigration policy in French Guyana (Calmont and Gorgeon 1987, Piantoni 2002, Zéphirin 2005) forced numerous new Haitian migrants who do not have siblings among the pioneers to come in under the family reunification policy to stay away from the border or to illegally entry. As a result, in their attempt to unlawfully cross the French Guyanese borders, they stop for a while at the fluvial region border (Saint-Laurent du Maroni) between Suriname and French Guyana. They settle themselves in towns and new urban neighborhoods in Suriname, where they organized a transitory way of living until they cross the border. As a matter of fact, the migrants associated with local populations build flimsy constructions, rent or sub-rent houses, and organize informal economic activities, which often are multiethnic.

The economic businesses are also supported by some social practices in terms of couple formations and mothers who give birth to children. These social and economic activities engender legal status of newborn babies with clandestine mothers. Often, while it is difficult for them to enter and stay in French Guyana, migrants cross both sides of the border to find sporadic jobs and manage their daily budget until they meet some legal and financial conditions to definitely move in French Guyana. Also, they are able (in some circumstances and some rare cases) to stop by Haiti for some reasons; after that, they return to Suriname—thus being illegal in both Suriname, the transit country, and in France (French Guyana), the destination

---

illegally through the frontier of Suriname. Since the end of 1980s, only 14 percent (or twenty-eight cases from fifty) of newcomers arrived by aircrafts at the Rochambeau's airport of Cayenne. Also, the eighteen cases that cross many neighboring countries' borders ought to be associated with the total number of 6,020 immigrants (passports) in the multipolar journey that, for access territory problems in the final destination (expelling or accompanied out of the border), chose to transit or make a detour on a neighboring territory for a period of time relatively long before reaching the targeted country of immigration. The eighteen cases of Haitian births on different loci of pause and transit on their migration routes also show up a form of living and a scattered legal identity on transnationalized borders in the inter-American space.

country. Such social, economic, and legal activities that Haitian migrants are involved in show the limitations of the physical border as a matter of efficiency policy (Haas and Czaika 2013, Czaika and Haas 2013) in controlling immigrations (Mitchell 1992, Miller 1994, Weiner 1995).

The administrative border symbolizing state sovereignty does not deter people-to-people cooperation, which sometimes, and under some circumstances, could go beyond the state intervention. Proximity in geography, the historical conditions, and the ethnic composition of populating neighboring inter-American countries set the stage for such a regional cooperation among neighboring countries and people. The various transnational socioeconomic practices not only question the border as a frontline of the state sovereignty, but more importantly, also reveal new parameters to put forth a cognitive conceptual dimension to the border as a specific part of a national sovereign territory, which is more appropriate to seize the complexity of personal relationships that neighboring peoples cultivate with a portion of a transnationalized territory. In this view, the interplay between people-to-people interaction and the borderland gave rise to a "border region," which, in its causes and effects, undermines the physical border as a simple frontline.

In other words, the temporary living and constructing flimsy houses with their various activities make sense of the concept of the "border region" that Zéphirin (2005, 2016) called *Guyaity*[48] as a neologism, which describes a more cognitive transnational territory created by people movements and cooperation across national borders (between Haiti, Suriname, and French Guyana) than a real judicial and politico-administrative one.

---

[48] A neologism that means French Guyana-Haiti territorial cognitive outbound and practices.

CARTE #1 :     Les points de départ, de transit et d'arrivée dans la multipolarité des déplacements d'Haïti en Guyane: De 2005 à nos jours.

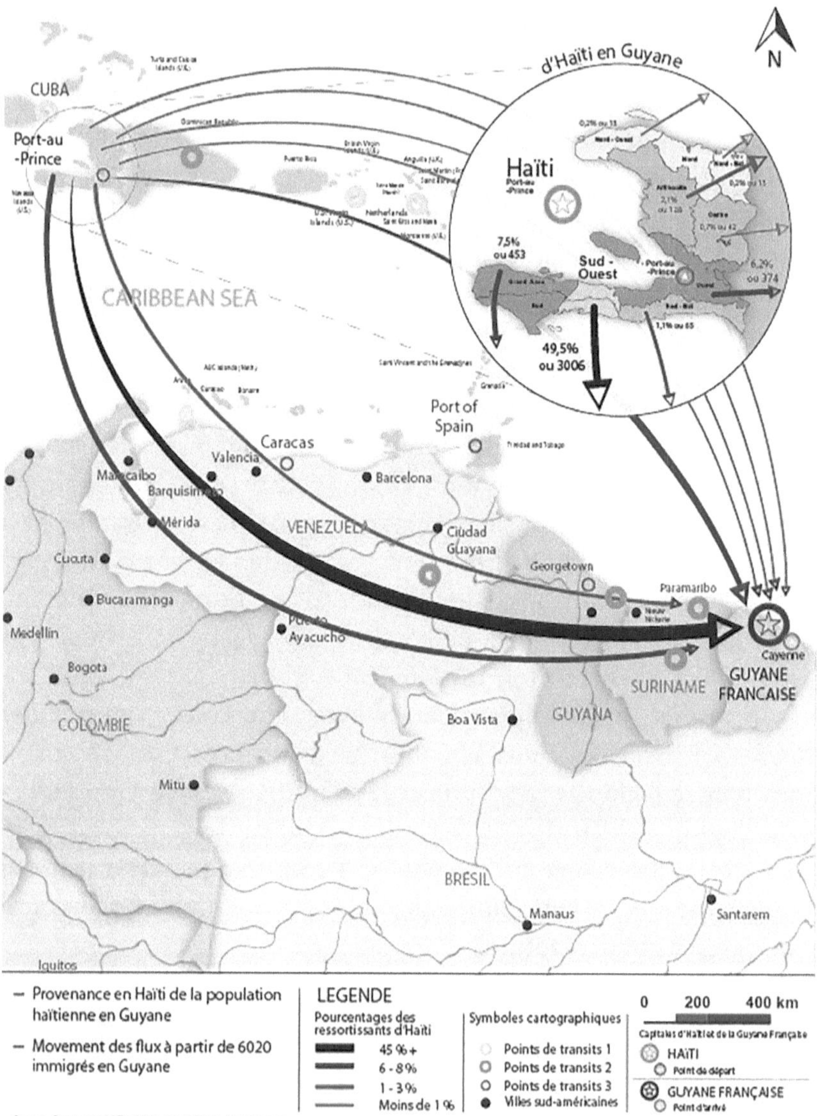

— Provenance en Haïti de la population haïtienne en Guyane

— Movement des flux à partir de 6020 immigrés en Guyane

LEGENDE

Pourcentages des ressortissants d'Haïti

- 45 % +
- 6 - 8%
- 1 - 3%
- Moins de 1 %

Symboles cartographiques

- Points de transits 1
- Points de transits 2
- Points de transits 3
- Villes sud-américaines

0    200    400 km

Capitales d'Haïti et de la Guyane Française

HAÏTI
Point de départ

GUYANE FRANÇAISE
Point d'arrivé

Source: Romanovski Zephirin 2005, Thèse de Doctorat

CARTE #2 :    La Guyane dans le système migratoire multi-polaire haïtien en Amériques    : De 2005 à nos jours

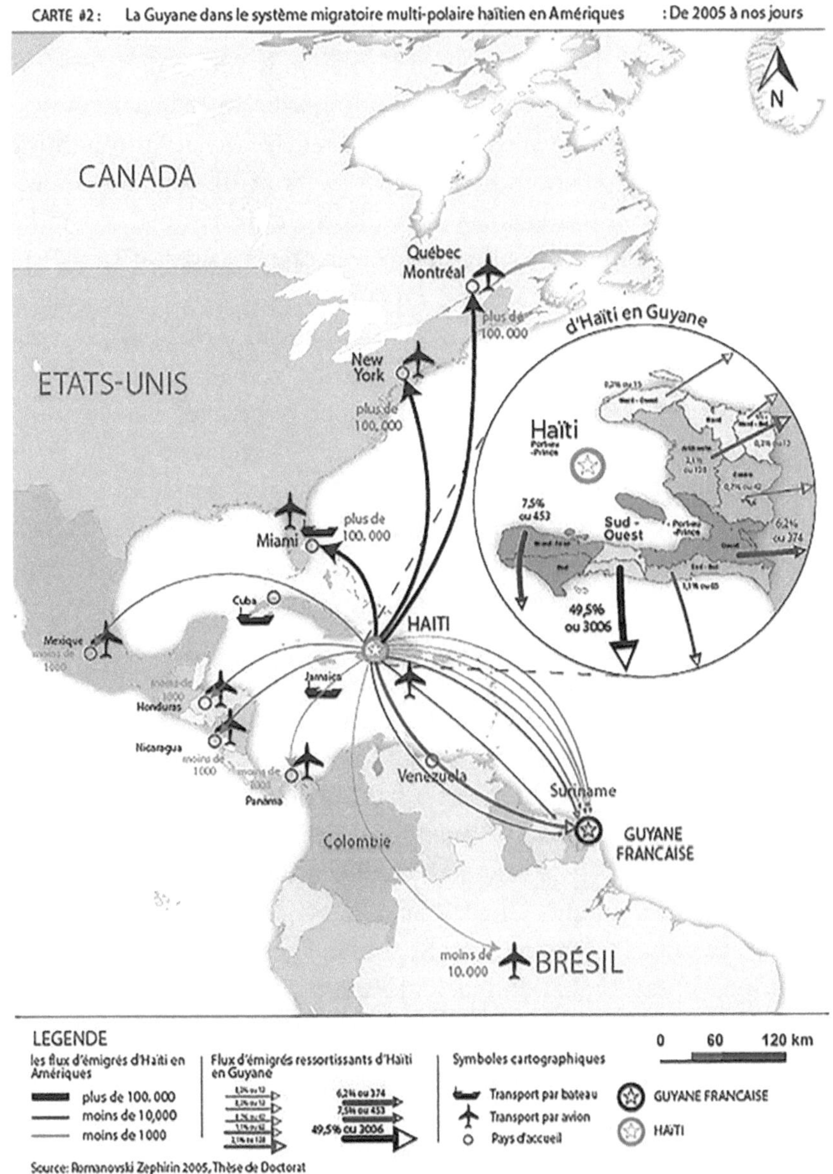


LEGENDE

les flux d'émigrés d'Haïti en Amériques

plus de 100.000
moins de 10,000
moins de 1000

Flux d'émigrés ressortissants d'Haïti en Guyane

0,2% ou 12
0,2% ou 12
0,7% ou 42
1,1% ou 65
2,1% ou 128
6,2% ou 374
7,5% ou 453
49,5% ou 3006

Symboles cartographiques

Transport par bateau
Transport par avion
Pays d'accueil

GUYANE FRANCAISE
HAïTI

0    60    120 km

Source: Romanovski Zephirin 2005, Thèse de Doctorat

The concrete practices of human mobility on scalar spaces and time change the perception of neighboring people of borders. The temporary "appropriation" of transborder loci redefines migrants-local populations' relationships with borderlands and materializes the transnationality by migrants' feet pounding in between loci. However, people movements between Haiti and French Guyana through the border of Suriname are more complex in terms of migrants' trajectories, routes, and strategies. As a result, the transnational territorial dimension in human mobility goes over one country of transit to include not only Suriname and French Guyana and, more importantly, to encompass multipolar inter-American territorial practices in neighboring countries (Zéphirin 2016).

Moreover, inter-American multipolar people movements[49] (Zéphirin 2009) through origin, transit, and destination countries as transnational territoriality connected to migrants' strategies and new routes undermine tightening border policy. In this view, the French Guyanese and Suriname fluvial border crossing and "border region" settlements are not in isolation with the Haitian migrants' strategies and routes in the whole Americas.

French Guyana is a part of a broader pattern of transnational displacements on the American continent involving in priority North, Central, and the Caribbean and South America. In other words, French Guyana becomes a part, a subsystem of the Haitian inter-American migration system (Zéphirin 2016). As such, it connects migrants' networks like the US through Florida, Canada (Montreal), Martinique, Guadeloupe, French Guyana, Saint-Martin, Cuba, Bahamas, Dominican Republic, Mexico, Brazil, Chile, Ecuador, Venezuela, Colombia, and Panama (Zéphirin 2018).

---

[49] In comparing data in the file of 6,020 Haitian passports and the results of fifty questionnaires, I come to term that the eighteen cases (from the total 6,020) are in close connection with the 72 percent zterviewed in the immigrant Haitian population and having at a certain point in time unlawfully reached French Guyana by stopping by the frontal zone of Saint-Laurent du Maroni. In other words, in themselves, the eighteen cases taken separately do not heavily weigh, but they manifest as problematic when considered in the frame of general multipolar displacements and irregular entries in Guyana.

The combined repulsive immigration policy and prohibited illegal entry push numerous Haitian migrants to transit or to stay definitely in many neighboring countries in the Americas. The frequency and the magnitude of the traditional human mobility coupled with casual forced migrations and refugee flows between Haiti and nearby inter-American (Smith 2001) countries crossing transnationalizing scales of territories engender more and more interstate dialogue and cooperation reflecting an evolution that shifts from a simple transnational matter to give way to a more bilateral and multilateral (Zéphirin 2016) diplomacy and immigration foreign policy in the Americas.

For instance, in the early 1990s, thousands of forced migrants and refugees fleeing a bloody military coup flooded many inter-American neighboring countries.

The influxes of refugees scaled up and impacted the different migration streams of Haitians in the Americas, which interacted one to another, and in their diverse causes and effects, they gave a regional inter-American dimension to the politico-migration crisis. The scale and scope of the migration crisis went over a simple transnational issue with the involvement of nonstate actors to cause specific statal foreign policies on entry rules, border crossing for forced migrants and refugees, and more importantly, to adopt a concerted coercive multilateral approach to overthrow the military regime and overcome the politico-migratory crisis.

In this broader regional strategy to curb refugees and forced migrations from Haiti, major multilateral organizations such as the OAS (the Organization of American States) and the UN teamed up to use (under the US military leadership in 1994) lethal forces against the Haitian source country of sending uncontrolled refuges and forced migrants across the Americas (Weiner 1995; Zéphirin 2005, 2016).

In other words, no matter the policy rationales either through attractive migration policy and legal entry or forced migrations, refugees and unwanted economic migrants both cause particular patterns (bipolar, linear, or scattered multipolar) of displacements in the

Americas and, more importantly, are amplifying factors of the transnational territoriality.

Haitian migrants on their way to Florida (the US) make stops sometimes in Cuba or in other neighboring islands. Recently, Brazil, Colombia, Panama and Mexico were added among many transitory steps leading to the priority destination that constitutes the United States. All these stops on the migration road create human links and sometimes humanitarian concerns in crossed transitory countries, which allow people-to-people transnational cooperation (with the good and the bad), often without state intervention.

Generally speaking, as abovementioned, the Haitian migration in French Guyana shows some significant changes. A private agro-industrial (Chalifaux 1988, Gallibourg 1995) plant and state infrastructural development projects injected an important amount of money in the economy. In this context, the pioneers, who came as migrant workers to fulfill available low- and mid-skilled jobs in both private and public sectors, presented through time many transformations. They (partly) moved from temporary guest workers and job seekers to entrepreneurs and employers. This socioeconomic shift in the status of many immigrants differently impacts capital mobility (Berstein and Weiner 1999) in both migrants' sending and receiving countries. The socioeconomic mutation of immigrants in their host country affects particularly immigrants' choices of investment, the country of investing, remittances patterns (Tapinos and Garson 1981, IADB 2007, Marcilli and Lowell 2005, Zéphirin 2012), and the length of the stay in the home country. The way of living on both sides of the migration stream often relates to the autonomous (De Gourcy 2005, Ma Mung 2009) willingness of integration and/ or reintegration (Costa-Lascoux 1999).

In this view, the choice to definitely settle in the host country and/or to move back in the home country generally sparks spatial footprint through housing construction practices, which, at some point, reveal a family transnationalization having its own transnational sociality. As a result, the Haitian-French Guyanese transnational movements in their causes and effects generate a conceptual shift of the border through the border-crossing practices of border crossers. In this context, the borderline (Jolivet 1989, Laethier 2011) undergoes borderland and "border region" (Lochack 1997, Piantoni 2002, Zéphirin 2005).

And in reaction to repulsive immigration policy (Weiner 1995, Bernstein and Weiner 1999), multipolar displacements allow irregular migrants to bypass and mitigate tightening border policy as unwanted immigrants look for new trajectories, routes, and strategies to migrate. Migrants' changing tactics on their way out to outmigration transform the linear and bipolar (Simon 1985, Massey et al. 1987, Massey 1993) trajectories into multipolar and scattered displacements all around the American continent (Zéphirin 2016). In other words, economic investments, money transfer, workers, and residential and human mobility that federate networks (Massey et al. 1998, Krissman 2005), scalar spaces, and levels of tansnationality (Sassen 1991, Sassen 1996, Robinson 2009) reverberate on housing, border crossing, and multipolar displacements in the Americas (Smith 2001, Zéphirin 2005).

The scale and the scope of the transnationality are a factor of local public policy, territorial formation, recomposition, and governance as both political geographies and geopolitics (Barton 2003) between Western Hemisphere countries (Stark 1998, Paquet 2005, Zéphirin 2016) and Haiti.

Definitely, from emigration, immigration, migrants to return migration processes (in their diverse factors and interrelated logics), transnational mobility of labor, capital, residence, and people in the inter-American space bring forth the mutational dimension in the directionality of migrants' influxes. The directionality issue in migration combined with scalar territorial trajectories, practices, and formation becomes in itself a system of loci in the transnational territoriality, which extends farther than Haiti and French Guyana. More importantly, they should be seen as part of the age of migration (Castle and Miller 2009) and regionalization-globalization (Sassen 1991, 1996; Stark 1998; Goldin 2006; Robinson 2009).

## Conclusion

To conclude, transnational living practices on both sides on the Haitian-French Guyanese migration stream spark public policy issues.

In French Guyana, the residential locations and relocations cause local public policy concerns. The urban areas that received the immigrants were built and organized in a way that could, at first, be of less interest for the state to intervene and regulate the distribution of units of dwellings. However, aside from the personal willingness of immigrants to live in cheaper urban neighborhoods in order to maximize their monthly income and pay less for housing, it is important to note that when urban territories are constituted outside the city extension plan and policy, new houses from immigrants become an important problem. It appears in urban planning, land-property law, public order, and safety issues.

As the urban population grows, locally elected mayors have to deal with different kinds of security concerns within and out the immigrant community. The many new constituted urban areas are unlawful and overcrowded, built in part on prone environmental disaster neighborhoods with risks of fire hazards and the incapacity for firefighters to easily enter and light off the blaze. However, the working population, in order to fulfill some important and abandoned jobs in the urban economy of French Guyana matters, needs to be housed, and for an affordable price. As a result, substandard dwellings in the city outskirts allow the immigrant workers to find a place to live.

Also, the pioneers established themselves in self-segregated urban areas in their first phase of settlement. However, with their integration, where they choose to definitely dwell in their host society (Touraine 1997), the pioneers sharply change their relationship with the territory and the houses as they redefine themselves as the human being in transition, carrying a dual or binational identity. In this view, the choice to relocate in the new urban neighborhoods generates also urban planning, land use, and environmental degradation concerns for both local and departmental authorities. Often, both segments of the French Guyanese politico-administrative body do not side on the line in terms of public policy rationales and processes.

While the French state in the overseas department tries to inclusively integrate everyone in the city planning (Zéphirin and Piantoni 2009) and make the affordable housing program as a means of alleviating poverty (Chuhan 2006) and reducing inequality, locally elected mayors tend to be selective for many reasons in the types of population they are willing to embrace in their strategy of local politics and public policy purposes (Zéphirin 2017a). Consequently, on the ground, a competing public policy divides major political parties on the hot-button issue of immigration.

And depending on the way that mainstream political parties approach the immigrants' integration or reintegration, it could differently impact the urban relocation in new town houses, the perception of the newly built space, the self, and the host society at large. Often, the institutional solutions, through local politics and municipal public policy, create new incentives for political incorporation and participation (Bueker 2005) and new interests for inclusively managing new network urban spaces.

As a result, immigrants relocate from segregated urban areas to a more multiethnic neighborhood in the Cayenne agglomeration. In its causes and effects, the urban relocation drives new political maps that redefine, at some point, local political landscapes, particularly at urban sectoral mayoral power in nearby cities and their urban segments within the Cayenne agglomeration.

Definitely, the shift both in the perception and in the practices of daily interconnected spaces becomes a factor of territorial formation and territoriality. The relationship among homeowners, the houses in their local urban territory, and the household's new sociality within the receiving society at different geographical scales show a convergence of social and economic interests of immigrants with other sectors of the local civil society. The intersected interests converge and reverberate on the local political scene, which ultimately produces new political geographies (Barton 2003) as urban segments and spatial scales evolve in a close interaction and interconnection.

In other words, living practices on urban land and territorial formation generating territoriality (Di Meo 1998) pertain public policy (Muller and Surel 1998, Friedberg 1997) principles in the host country. However, this phenomenon does not relate only to one side of the migration stream. It is a double-sided issue with transnational consequences. As a result, Haiti is also touched by the transnational territoriality through return migrants' housing constructions and social practices as public policy and territorial governance issues.

In southwestern Haiti, return migrants' settlements in the commune of Fond-des-Nègres create the same problems observed in French Guyana (Moreau 1999, DDE-Cayenne 1998, DDE-Cayenne 2001, Zéphirin and Piantoni 2009). However, unlike French Guyana, the weakness of the state in Haiti complicates and worsens the resettlement process. Money transfer grows as housing constructions are booming everywhere. The new houses correspond with migrants' dream of returning home to live in a big and nice house with their close family (which sometimes could include some close friends who, at some degree, are considered as extended family members).

However, the flawed institutional conditions of the country complicate the resettlement and show local politics and public policy (Muller and Surel 1998, Bueker 2005) structural limitations and crisis. The institutional impediment reverberates on the space management and territorial governance (Zéphirin 2005) in the communes facing a large extent of return migrations within Miragoane-Desruisseaux, Fond-des-Nègres, Aquin and (to a lesser extent) Saint-Louis-du-Sud. In terms of urbanism and urban policy (Brunet 1990, Roncayolo 1997, Rossi and Eisenmann 1999, Pinson 2000), a true vacuum characterizes the commune of Fond-des-Nègres. Local elected leaders are incompetent and outclassed by the issue of efficient local urban governance and planning.

An accelerating rural urbanization takes place without the constitution of a formal city and an urban policy planning. The rapid growth of the stock of newly built houses on agricultural lands does not go without environmental degradation (Domenach and Picouet 2001). Deforestation erodes the inclined lands and creates ravines on surrounding highlands. The deterioration in the natural environment and its vulnerability consequential to human actions combined with the variability of extreme weather events spark often sectoral flooding in low-lying areas in Fond-des-Nègres. In other words, the natural environmental security issue does not locally cause a particular urban and housing public policy to address the fast-growing stock of newly built private homes in the wake of return migration processes. Contrary to French Guyana, locally elected mayors in southern Haiti are not equipped to set sustainability principles as an urban policy driver to redraw and extend the settlement area of new returning migrants in private family homes.

As a matter of fact, if in French Guyana, the integration process in private and public urban houses was accompanied by public institutions through diverse competing public policy approaches (Zéphirin and Piantoni 2008, Zéphirin 2009), in Haiti, where modern local territorial governance is quasi inexistent, public policy has a long way to go before becoming effective, efficient, and inclusive in order to institutionally face the rural urbanization crisis as an opportunity to set a new urban planning project.

The poorly governed communal territories, urban sectors, and towns in Haiti received a countless amount of money from their expatriates to family members living in the home country. In spite of migrants' remittances, which are registered in many localities (Zéphirin 2008, 2014, 2016), public space and new human settlements are still (Roncayolo 1997, Pinson 2000) underserved in terms of public management. Consequently, the lack of financial resources, which is too often associated with poverty and emerging shantytowns, is an argument that cannot be strongly supported in regard to the fact that, to a large extent, homeowners in Fond-des-Nègres (Southwest Haiti) build their private homes from transferred hard currencies such as the euro and the US dollar and the Canadian dollar. The capacity of the local municipal governments to set policy principles and benchmarks to deal with socioeconomic spatial integration or reintegration on both sides of the migration stream is crucial to tackle the interplay of human, land, and the environment at large. That purpose cannot be successfully achieved without a clear policy rationale and a public policy framework based on a sharp understanding of the human settlement in houses and urban relocation on both sides of the French Guyanese and Haitian migration stream.

As a matter of fact, emigration, immigration, and return migration processes engender conditions for both sending and receiving countries of migrants through bilateral channels of cooperation, sharing knowledge, and practices in public policy design and implementation as a way of better managing new political geographies, territories, and territoriality caused by transnational people movements.

Also, as the linear displacement patterns change through time into a multipolar one (consequential of national immigration policy) in the Western Hemisphere (Mitchell 1992), it becomes obvious that there is a shift in interstate cooperation on migration that moves from a bilateral to a more multilateral standpoint.

This new dimension would recalibrate the amplitude and the frequency of transnational people movements, not only in terms of territories, territoriality, and political geographies at a bilateral scale, but also in terms of scattered multipolar border crossing, inter-American migration system (Smith 2001), and its segments in subregions in the Americas. As a matter of fact, the shift from attractive to repulsive immigration policy affects transnational territories and territoriality through border crossers' practices of front lines bridging border regions until they end up reaching their final destination. Migrants' strategies to some degree undermine tightening border policies. They create new trajectories and routes that transcend state national politics and policy toward migrants (Zéphirin 2017a, 2017b) and, more importantly, interstate cooperation and management of unwanted immigrants or refugee flows.

In this view, all the necessary conditions are in place to raise the interrelated issues of migrants, border crossers, transnational territorial practices, entry rules, and nation-state involvements as a geopolitical sphere of influence. When displacements include origin, third, and host countries and the variability of influxes causing controlling border (Miller 1994, Lochack 1997) and entry policy on the one hand, and the constitution of stocks of unwanted foreign populations sparking absorption and human rights issues in neighboring countries on the second hand, these factors pave the way for a more multilateral cooperation and diplomacy (Zéphirin 2016).

In this view, in the past decades, Haitians' multipolar migrations and refugee flows draw particular geopolitics, where major political players (very influential countries) in the Western Hemisphere jointly used military force in 1994 to deter unwanted immigrants within their national borders. This is a matter of foreign policy in the region affecting Haiti's internal political regime change, but not limited to.

As a result, the Haitian French Guyanese migration, which shows residential mobility on scalar territories, drives political geographies. In fact, as immigrants in the long term are torn between integration and/or reintegration, they differently experience interrelated factors of labor, capital, human, and residential mobility. In this context, the bipolar migration network between Haiti and French Guyana has shifted into a multipolar one connecting with larger international migration networks crossing the whole inter-American space as an interactive migration system. This pertinent mutation of the Haitian French Guyanese migrations raises some theoretical questions and limitations about the strength of the "push-pull" factors alone to fully explain new actors, geographical scales, socioeconomic behaviors, and socio-spatial practices as a way of integration-reintegration in the migrant network. In consequence, it matters to explore the problematic margins, the interaction, and the interconnection between migrant network (Massey et al. 1987, 1993; Krissman 2005) and international migration networks (Zéphirin 2005) as a means of understanding and explaining multipolar transnational spaces (Zéphirin 2016) in political geographies[50] (Barton 2003) and geopolitics in the Americas.

The complex transnational human mobility as a reversibility (Domenach and Picouet 1997) dimension in the migration process

---

[50] Briefly, political geography as a subfield in human geography refers to human governments, border issues, subdivisions of political units, power, and territory in cities.

between French Guyana and Haiti, which transcends the whole Americas raises some more theoretical preoccupations in regard to the autonomy[51] theory (De Gourcy 2005; Ma Mung 2009, 3, 4, 5) in both mobility and migration studies. At a glance, the autonomy theory, in opposition to classical accounts, moves away from the two main approaches (Ma Mung 2009, 2, 3) of "mechanist approach" (emphasizing on the causes of geographical mobilities at macro scale) and a "diffusionist approach" (relying on the conditions of possibility for migrations at micro scale) to explore the *meso* level and focusing on personal initiatives in crafting voluntary migration project.

The transnationality in mobility and reversible migrations go over the mutually exclusive approach of causal alternative versus conditions of possibility or the antagonistic approach of macro versus micro geographic space, or also, spatial distance versus spatial sentiment belonging. These approaches are severely criticized by Ma Mung (2009) for their theoretical limitations in dealing with autonomous and voluntary decision-making to migrate or to craft a migration project, in spite of presenting at some point some pertinences in explaining international immigrations.

However, in regard to transnational mobility and reversibility (Domenach and Picouet 1995) in migrations, my own findings (Zéphirin 2005, 2016) reveal that not only the cause and effect relations are not consubstantially and necessarily exclusive, in some particular cases they are interacted and/or inversed[52] (Domenach 1996, 75) factors in transnational people movements (Zéphirin 2008), but more importantly, Ma Mung's (2009) theoretical "autonomy approach" in migration is considered as relevant only in analyzing the transnational reversibility dimension of migration and not as a fully pertinent account to explain international migrations.

---

[51] Generally speaking, the "autonomy" account reports to "knowledge, know-how, self-referent, action, practices, affirmation, differentiation, interaction, internal voluntary initiative of individuals taken personally and/or collectively."

[52] Aside from the semantic aspect, different interrelated and inversed factors involved in migration events move from "cause to effect" on the one hand to "both cause and effect" on the second hand.

My findings (Zéphirin 2005, 2016) show first transnational mobility as a means of reversibility, associates and merges the dualist approach of external conditions and personal and internal initiative. Second, if the discrepancy appears among macro and micro geographical scales, the spatial distance, and the spatial sentiment belonging weigh significantly in the implementation of the emigration project. However, in the transnational return migrations, the differences among macro/micro scales, spatial distance, and spatial sentiment belonging are compounded in the reversibility process in housing constructions and social practices of spatial trajectories in transnational residences.

The external conditions to the internal-personal decision-making, prefiguring the return migrations in the home country not only are not necessarily contradictory but are complementary factors (at some point) in human transnational mobility and reversibility in houses spatially distributed. However, once installed in the host country, despite the voluntary decision to return, some external conditions to the "remigrants" at home could relativize their returning choices and end up pushing them back to their old host country in a kind of endless migration (Domenach and Picouet 1995, Zéphirin 2005) where often, the constructed houses are sold.

According to Zéphirin (2016), the "autonomy" is seen more as a reversibility facet in migration addressing individual or grouping migrants' strategies (within their host country) to return home than a fully relevant theoretical approach as framed by Ma Mung (2009) to explain international migrations in its diverse phases of moving from home to arriving to host countries and also returning. Mobility as a means of reversibility reveals grounded evidences that migrants' concrete autonomous initiatives and socio-spatial practices of houses. Migrants' voluntary strategies overpass the simple theoretical cause-and-effect factors (attraction-repulsion) to link both immigration and return migration rationales and projects in receiving and sending countries.

Migrants, through their individual and/or collective projects, evolve on the long term. Their evolution reflects their personal history, trajectories, spatial strategies, and socioeconomic practices that deeply reverberate on their migration project[53] (Zéphirin 2005, Ma Mung 2009). As a result, complex interrelated (objective and subjective) factors shift the initial initiative to voluntary migrate from temporary to definitive or to return migration or to an endless migration. In other words, the mutation of the migration project concerning legal status, urban land ownership, urban relocation, and home ownership seriously impacts the diverse forms of mobility, often taking place in an interactive network of transnational loci. The change in the migration project from the host society to the origin one, in practice, gums up together socio-spatial, scalar, and spatial belonging sentiment.

Return migrations, dual or secondary private family houses on poly-loci and the periodicity in the use of houses (according to occupational activities, semi-retirement or retirement), leave their marks on the transnationalization of the sociality of scattered families who are periodically reunified. These socio-spatial and transnational practices go through and bridge spatial, external conditions, and internal personal factors to shape the forms of mobility, reversibility, and more importantly the migration project.

The combination of migrants' remittances, housing constructions, social practices on transnational loci, and urban relocation stands out the voluntary human mobility. Residences are moving from one particular neighborhood to another, often from an ethnically and self-segregated urban area to a more multicultural urban segment. In some degree, voluntary urban relocation or permanent urban settlements prefigure a change in the migration project, which is torn between integration and/or reintegration.

The migration project has historically and autonomously shaped the interaction of distinct urban segments by voluntary decision-making and personal initiatives within the immigrant commu-

---

[53] Migration project is used as an analyzing tool in migration studies. It emphasizes on migrants' life, their diverse and interrelated practices, perceptions, possibilities, and opportunities, rather than determinants and causes. Migration project intersects with migrants' biographies, civil or legal status, personal history, trajectories, territorial belonging sentiments, initiative capacity, and empowerment.

nity, revealing a process of urban-rural production on both sides of the migration stream in regard to key tendencies of integration-reintegration. The gathered evidences brought forth by Zéphirin (2005, 2016) on the mobility as a means of reversibility and transnational territories intersect at some point with the autonomy theory (De Gourcy 2005, Ma Mung 2009) in migration. Transnational complex practices connected to both the evolution of the migration project and migrants' autonomous strategies in reversibility stand out, competing tendencies of voluntary integration-reintegration (Zéphirin and Piantoni 2009), individual initiatives, collective strategies, affirmed actions that both differ and interact individuals, families, groups, and the community. These strategies (in their diverse causes and effects) are federated on a hierarchy of spaces created from internal determinants within the immigrant community installed and deployed in French Guyana and transnationalized in Haiti.

The "autonomy" (De Gourcy 2005, Ma Mung 2009) in migrants' decision-making to migrate by prioritizing internal and personal dispositions consequentially excludes external determinants in analyzing migrants' transnational mobility through their migration project and migrants' spatial production (Zéphirin 2005).

In this view, while being partly critiqued toward the autonomy theoretical account in analyzing international migrations, my findings (Zéphirin 2016) in some measure side with the "autonomy" theory on already well-established immigrant communities or internal migrations.

In this chapter, the analysis of transnational mobility and reversibility of migrants purposively, which reframes the concept of "autonomy," refers to it mainly in specific aspects of an already internally deployed immigrant population, personal, collective, and voluntary migrants' initiatives, housing practices, urban relocation strategies, and socio-spatial trajectories as a means of both shaping the migration project and socio-spatial production and does absolutely not report to an explicative theory of international migrations (De Gourcy 2005, Ma Mung 2009).

If I partly agree with the "autonomy theory," in migration studies, it only concerns the second face of the human mobility or return migrations where an already settled population spatially strategizes to spread in and shape the host country's urban structure, which faces key tendencies of integration-reintegration.

However, I strongly disagree with the "autonomy theory" in terms of transnational mobility and international migrations for overemphasizing on internal dispositions and personal initiatives (in an immigrant community), which are mutually exclusive of external determinants drawing migrations. Once again, my own grounded evidences (Zéphirin 2005, 2016) point out that crossing borders or entry to territory as a means of immigration policy (influx of people) does not line at all with the "autonomy theory" principles in dealing with the various institutional and political diverse actors (to citing a few) on geographical hierarchical scales before an international migration event gets achieved from north-to-south or from south-to-south people movements. On this matter, the "autonomy theory" is very limited to highlight complex and interrelated factors regarding transnational human mobility, reversible migrations, and immigration policy efficiency (Czaika and Hass 2013).

Furthermore, the socio-spatial practices in houses between French Guyana and Haiti show a geo-sociology of transnationality. As a result, according to the fact that the multipolarity in migrants' displacements in the Americas breaks down the migrant's network and its traditional barriers in favor of larger interconnections in regional international migration networks (Zéphirin 2018), and the Western Hemisphere during the 1990s moves toward economic regionalization[54] and sub-regionalization (Stark 1998, Paquet 2005), it becomes crucial to problematically reframe the geo-sociology of transnationality of migration into a broader perspective of the sociology of globalization (Sassen 1991, 2007; Robinson 2009) where transnational migration, labor, and capital mobility (Sassen 1988) within urban network systems play a key role.

---

[54] Allowing influxes of goods, money, and people to cross national borders.

The migrants' transnational territoriality raises inter-American reversible migrations as an issue of the regionalized-globalized[55] (Robinson 2009, 7) economy in the Western Hemisphere. If authors such as Sassen Saskia (1991, 1996) and Robinson (2009) defend the view that globalization connects various spatial categories and becomes a process that restructures spaces and places, through a transnationalized population who reorganized their spatial relations from local to global scales, they both mainly based their works on transnational migration from southern poor to northern rich countries and their integration in urban margins in global cities, or they refer to some southern low- or middle-income countries with the penetration of global investment funds in cities, producing disruptive effects on rural areas.

However, they (Sassen 1991, 1996; Robinson 2009) quasi neglect the reversible dimension of immigrations from global cities to rural territories or to southern countries, causing important destructuring-restructuring territorial effects with informal influxes of money from migrants' remittances. Thus, without formal private investment funds from the global economy in cities, southern countries and their territories are considerably affected. As a matter of fact, the Haitian-French Guyanese migration stream, which is interconnected with other inter-American reversible migration currents, disorganizes-reorganizes de facto various spatial scales. At some point,

---

[55] Referring to Sassen Saskia's work (1988) the *Mobility of Capital and Labor*, Robinson (2009, 7) wrote,

> Two processes associated with globalization [from a political-economy approach], but traditionally treated as separate phenomena: the transnationalization of production and the transnational migration of labor.
>
> Globalization is based on networks of global cities connected by a digitalized infrastructure and involving new transnational flown of people, power and culture... Globalization redefines the relationship between production and territoriality, economic organization, institutions and social processes.

this spatial mutation questions the traditional national hierarchy of urban territories in relation with their countryside.

Rural territories become, in practice (for some villages in Haiti, not all, and for many reasons like differentials in migration patterns and tendencies), more connected to global cities in the Western Hemisphere (like New York, Boston, Miami, Montreal, in a lesser extent to Cayenne, Sao Paulo in Brazil, and Santiago in Chile) than some small-, mid-, or large-sized cities in Haiti; thus, paradoxically, without a big penetration of the formal global investment capital central for the economic globalization. The geographical proximity of Haiti with some key "urban command centers" of the globalization (Sassen 1991, Robinson 2009) in the Americas allows the country to be (informally or indirectly) affected by influxes of return migrants, goods, and money, unlike the Dominican Republic, which has at some point some global capital investment from some major command centers (largely the United States) of the global economy. In other words, it becomes important to consider the reversibility and the transnational territoriality as lacking dimensions of the transnational migration, so crucial for the economic regionalization and globalization through the strategy of free trade, comparative advantage, cheap labor market, and production of consumer goods.

Voluntary reversible migrations (Domenach 1995, Zéphirin 2016) in their causes and effects on transnational territories and territoriality (Di Meo 1997) impact the debate over whether old peripheral territories (in the world economy) or new "command centers" (in the globalization) are connected to global cities. More importantly, the multipolarity in both migrations and return migrations shows, at some point, the discrepancy in levels of development in Western Hemisphere countries and their different options in favor or against meeting readiness principles or stayed confined in reluctance toward economic regionalization and globalization (Paquet 2005).

Haiti, with a weak state (falling into state failing) and facing return migrations, is experiencing new emerging and fast-growing urbanized territories in rural areas. In their socioeconomic causes and effects, they spark some kind of new poverty and inequality in terms of access to decent private housing and satisfying other basic human needs. Partly, global money as migrants' remittances is circulating in Haiti's rural areas like Fond-des-Nègres and other villages. In consequence, multipolar return migrations and their transnationalized populations lay out a double standard of living conditions in rural areas where global patterns of the way of living are found and coexist with traditional and archaic forms of living.

To some degree, the transnationalized populations are connected to the transnational urban systems of some globalized economic "command centers." Consequently, north-south or south-south return migrations, alongside transnational migrations in global urban centers, have to be integrated in scholars' globalization studies and research agendas in order to better cover some unseen aspects in the interplay of globalization-migration, return migrations, and transnationalized territories as a means of globality[56] (Robinson 2009, 6) or the emerging global-regional territoriality formation.

Obviously, within host countries, immigrants point out particular spatial logics, correlated to their socioeconomic conditions, practices of their host cities in a way that presupposes a personal trajectory (a migratory biography), leading to a reversible migration project. According to their voluntary project of integration or reintegration (not necessarily mutually exclusive) in places and spaces of the host or origin country, immigrants live and appropriate cities differently and develop particular socio-spatial relations in interconnected network transnationalized territories.

This geo-sociology of transnationality and its rationales are mainly revealed by the reversible migration project in both host cities and origin rural-urban areas of migrants. Focusing blindly on one receiving side of immigrants in urban systems will not allow to understand the whole picture of the transnational migrations and reversible migrations in cities or analyzing disruptive effects in origin local-rural communities.

Definitely, in regard to the central research-guided question, labor, capital, human, and residential mobility in their interactions

---

[56] "Various specific, often localized processes, so that there is no real encompassing overview of global processes or a theoretical conception of globality."

between French Guyana and Haiti transcend borderlines to shape borderlands and border regions through border crossers' trajectories. As a result, if in the short term the immigrant community has been constituted by interrelated "push-pull" factors, in the long term, diverse mutations and new practices in labor, money transfer, human, and residential mobility transform and split immigrants between two great tendencies of integration and reintegration, showing a human voluntary factor through autonomous initiatives that shape the migration project itself. Immigrants' autonomous and personal decision imposes itself as a voluntary dimension of migration reversibility.

This voluntary and autonomous parameter is forgotten by the "push-pull" factors that were theoretically relevant on the short-term constitution of the immigrant community, but irrelevant on the long term to highlight personal initiatives' importance regarding returning migration processes and their multiple causes and effects. More importantly, the combination of diverse practices and actors' rationales on various spatial scales pertains to territorial production, transnational territoriality, and political geographies in the specific Haitian-French Guyanese bipolar subsystem connected to the broader multipolar inter-American migration space system.

Now, more importantly, this perspective raises the need to scholars' globalization studies research agenda to pay a closer attention to transnationality and territoriality issues as a means of regionality and "globality" in an age of migration (Castle and Miller 2011). It requires to interact migrants' networks (Massey et al. 1987, Krissman 2005) with international migration networks to problematize the inter-American space (Smith 2001; Zéphirin 2005, 2016, 2018) as a migration system (and subsystems) while exploring linkages between transnational migrations and autonomous reversible migration strategies and their impacts on host and origin cities and territorial formation. Such a research object would give a better problematic insight in interacting bipolar and multipolar migration studies in the broader context of economic regionalization-globalization (Sassen 1991, 1996; Robinson 2009).

# References


Barton, Jonathan R. 2003. *A Political Geography of Latin America* (ebook*).* London: Taylor and Francis.

Bernstein, Ann and Myron Weiner. 1999. *Migration and Refugee Policies. An Overview.* New York: Continuum.

Bueker, Catherine, Simpson. 2005. "Political Incorporation among Immigrants from Ten Areas of Origin: The Persistence of Source Country Effects." *International Migration Review* (*IMR*) 39, no.1 (Spring): 103–140.

Brunet, Roger. 1990. *Le territoire dans les turbulences.* Montpellier: Reclus.

Calmont, Régime and Catherine Gorgeon. 1987. L'immigration haïtienne en Guyane. *Equinoxe, Centre Guyanais d'Etudes et de Recherche (CEGER)*, no. 23: 1–16.

Castle, Stephen and Mark J. Miller. 2009. *The Age of Migration: International Population Movements in the Modern World.* New York: Palgrave.

Castor, Elie and Georges Othilly. 1984. La Guyane: Les grands problèmes, les solutions possibles. Paris: Caraïbes Editions.

Costa-Lascoux, Jacqueline. 1999. L'intégration à la française: une philosophie des lois. In Dewitte Philippe (Ed.), *Immigration et intégration, l'état des savoirs:* 328–339. Paris: La Découverte.

Czaika, Mathias and Hein de Haas. 2013. "On the Effectiveness of Immigration Policies," in *Population and Development Review*: 487–508.

Chalifaux, Jean-Jacques. 1988. *Chercher la vie en Guyane française. Témoignages d'Haïtiens et d'Haïtiennes émigrés.* Laval: Département d'Anthropologie, Université de Laval-Québec.

Chantilly, Hector. 1980. Effets du centre spatial guyanais sur le développement économique et l'emploi en Guyane, l'économie guyanaise et l'emploi en 1980: bilan et perspectives. In *Revue La Réalité*, no 5. (October): 1–19.

Chuhan, Punam. 2006. Poverty and Inequality. In Vinay. Bhargava. (Ed.). *Global Issues for Global Citizens:* 31–50. Washington, DC: The World Bank.

DDE-Cayenne. 1998. *Etude urbaine et socio-économique des phéno-mènes de l'habitat informel sur le littoral de Guyane. Les territoires de l'exclusion* (tome 1 et 2). Cayenne: Ministère de l'Equipement, des Transports et du Logement-Direction Départementale de l'Equipement de la Guyane (Octobre).

DDE-Cayenne. 2001. PDALPD—*Plan départemental d'action logement aux personnes défavorisées, 1992–1998, 1999–2001.* Cayenne: DDE.

De Gourcy, Constance. 2005. *L'autonomie dans la migration. Réflexion autour d'une énigme. Paris:* L'harmattan (Collection Logiques sociales).

de Haas, Hein and Mathias Czaika. 2013. "Measuring Policies: Some Conceptual and Methodological Reflections." In *Migration and Citizenship* 1, no.2 (Summer): 40–47.

Di Meo, Guy. 1998. *Géographie sociale et territoire.* Paris: Nathan Université.

Domenach, Hervé and Michel Picouet 1995. *Les Migrations. Paris:* Que Sais-Je? PUF.

Domenach, Hervé. 1996. "De la migratologie," *Revue Européenne des Migrations Internationales* 12, no. 2: 73–86.

Domenach, Hervé and Michel Picouet. 2004. Population, Environnement et Développement. La durabilité en question. Paris: L'Harmattan.

Friedberg, Erhard. 1997. *Le pouvoir et la règle. Dynamique de l'action organisée.* Paris Seuil.

Gallibourg, Eric. 1995. *L'accès à l'habitat. Le cas des immigrés haï-tiens en Guyane française.* Université de Bordeaux II, Maison des sciences de l'homme d'Aquitaine, Programme PIR ville, Rapport intermédiaire Tome 1, Tome 2 (Annexes), Mars.

Girault, A. Christian. 1975. "Nouvelles données sur l'économie haï-tienne." In *La Documentation française. Notes et études documen-taires,* no. 4190–4191, 22 Mai: 39–41.

Golding, Ian. 2006. "Globalizing with their feet: The Opportunities and Costs of International Migration." In Vinay, Barghava. (Ed.). *Global Issues for Global Citizens:* 105–121. Washington, DC: World Bank Report.

IADB. Inter-American Development Bank. 2007. *Haiti Remittance Survey*. Port-au-Prince www.iadb.org.pdf.

INSEE-TER. 2003. *Tableaux Economiques Régionaux*. Guyane-Cayenne.

INSEE-TER. 2006. *Tableaux Economiques Régionaux*: Guyane-Cayenne.

Jolivet, Marie-José. 1989. Introduction à la question des ethnies et des frontières en Guyane française. In Jolivet, Marie-José. (Ed). *Question d'identités comparées:* 117–132. Paris: ORSTOM.

Krissman, Fred. 2005. "Sin Coyote ni Patron: Why the Migrant Network Fails to Explain International Migration." *International Migration Review (IMR)* 39, no. 1 (Spring): 4–44.

Laethier, Maud. 2011. "Le Surinam, passages vers la Guyane. D'un pays à l'autre dans la circulation migratoire des Haïtiens." *Cahiers de l'Urmis*, on the Internet at (http://urmis.revues. org/951) 7, no. 2:1–14.

Lochack, Daniele. 1997. La fermeture des frontières ne peut tenir lieu de politique, *Migrations-Société*, no. 50–51 (Mars-Avril): 5–9.

Ma Mung, Emmanuel. 2009. "Le point de vue de l'autonomie dans l'étude des migrations internationales: penser de l'intérieur les phénomènes de mobilité." In Françoise Dureau; Marie-Antoinette Hily. *Les mondes de la mobilité: 25–38. Rennes:* Presses de l'Université de Rennes.

Mam-Lam-Fouk, Serge. 1997. *L'identité guyanaise en question. Les dynamiques interculturelles en Guyane* française. Kourou: Ibis rouge.

Marcilli, A. E. and B. L. Lowell. 2005. "Transnational Twist: Pecuinary Remittances and the Socioeconomic Integration of Authorized and Unauthorized Mexican Immigrants in Los Angeles County." *International Migration Review (IMR)* 39, no. 1 (Spring): 69–102.

Massey, S. Douglas et al. 1987. *Return to Aztlan: The Social Process of International Migration from Western Mexico*. Berkeley: University of California.

Massey, Douglas. 1993. Theories of International Migration, *Population and Development Review* 19 (3).

Miller, Mark J. 1994. "Introducing the Critical Transparency School of Immigration Analysis." In Wayne A. Cornélius., Philip L. Martin., and James F. Hollifield (eds.). *Controlling Immigration. A Global Perspective:* 107–112. California: Stanford University Press.

Mitchell, Christopher. 1992. *Western Hemisphere Immigration and United States Foreign Policy.* Ed. C. Mitchell. Pennsylvania: The Pennsylvania State University Press.

Muller, Pierre and Yves Surel. 1998. *L'Analyse des politiques publiques.* Paris: Monchrestien.

Moreau, Jean-Michel. 1999. *De la ville dessinée à la ville spontanée.* Cayenne: ARUAG (Agence Régionale d'Urbanisme et d'Aménagement de la Guyane), Mars.

Paquet, Gilles. 2005. *The New Geo-Governance. A Baroquie Approach.* Ottawa: University of Ottawa Press.

Piantoni, Frédéric. 2002. *Pouvoir national et acteurs locaux: L'enjeu des mobilités dans un espace en marge. Le cas de la Guyane française.* Poitiers: Thèse pour le doctorat de géographie, sous la direction de Simon Gildas, Université de Poitiers, UFR des Sciences Humaines et Arts, Département de géographie 5 janvier.

Pinson, Daniel. 2000. "Projet de ville et projets de vie." In Hayot d'Alain and Sauvage André (Ed.), *Le projet urbain. Enjeux, expérimentations et professions.* Paris: Editions de la Villette.

Robinson, William I. 2009. "Saskia Sassen and the Sociology of Globalization: A critical Appraisal." In *Sociological Analysis* 3, no. 1 (Spring).

Roncayolo, Marcel. 1997. *La ville et ses territoires.* Paris: Gallimard.

Rossi, Aldo and Peter Eisenman. 1999. *The Architecture of the City.* Cambridge: The Institute for Architecture and Urban Studies and the Massachusetts Institute of Technology, Tenth Printing.

Sassen, Saskia. 1991. *The Global City.* New York: Princeton University Press.

Sassen, Saskia. 1996. *Losing Control? Sovereignty in an Age of Globalisation.* New York: Columbia University Press.

Sassen, Saskia. 1988. *The Mobility of Capital and Labor: A Study in International Investment and Labor Flow*. Cambridge: Cambridge University Press.

Sassen, Saskia. 2007. *A Sociology of Globalization*. New York: W. W. Norton.

Simon, Gildas. 1985. *L'espace des travailleurs tunisiens en France: structures et fonctionnement d'un champ migratoire international*. Ed. G. Simon. Poitiers: Université de Poitiers.

Smith, C. Robert. 2001. "Current Dilemmas and Future Prospects of the Inter-American Migration System." In A. R. Zolberg and P. M. Benda (Ed.), *Global Migrants Global Refugees. Problems and solutions*: 121–167. New York: Berghahn Books.

Stark, Jeffrey. 1998. "Globalization and Democracy in Latin America." In *Fault Lines of Democracy in Post-Transition Latin America*: 67–96. Edited by Felipe Aguero and Jeffrey Stark. Miami: North-South Center Press at the University of Miami.

Tapinos, G. and Jean P. Garson. 1981. *L'Argent des immigrés: Revenus, épargne et transferts de huit nationalités immigrées en France*. Paris: PUF, INED.

Touraine, Alain. 1997. *Pourrons-nous vivre ensemble? Égaux et différents*. Paris: Fayard.

Weiner, Myron. 1995. *The Global Migration Crisis. Challenge to States and to Human Rights*. New York: Harper Collins.

Zéphirin, Romanovski. 2005. *Le Champ migratoire haïtiano-guyanais: étude des causes et effets politiques, socio-économiques et spatiaux. Multipolarité et réversibilité dans le système migratoire interaméricain*. Aix-en-Provence: Thèse de Doctorat sous la direction de Hervé Domenach, Université Aix-Marseille III, Faculté de Droit, d'Economie et des Sciences-IUAR (Institut d'Urbanisme et d'Aménagement Régional).

Zéphirin, Romanovski. 2008. "L'émigration-rémigration des Haïtiens dans l'espace interaméricain comme fin du modèle sociétal du pays en dehors—Repenser le développement," *Revue Migrations-Société*, vol. 20, no. 117–118, mai-août: 11–24.

Zéphirin, Romanovski and Frédéric Piantoni. 2009. "Les stratégies d'accès au logement des Haïtiens dans l'agglomération de

Cayenne comme facteurs de restructuration urbaine." In *Revue L'Espace Politique*, vol. 6. no. 3. Mai: 1–12. En ligne, www.l'espacepolitique.revues.org

Zéphirin phirin, Romanovski. 2012. "Transferts d'argent des migrants haïtiano-guyanais dans la multipolarité de l'espace américain." In *Revue Migrations Société* 24, no. 143 (Septembre–Octobre): 33–49.

Zéphirin, Romanovski. 2014. "Exploring the Role of Migrants' Remittances in the UN's Nation Building and Development Management in Haiti." In *Development in Practice* 24, no. 3: 420–434.

Zéphirin, Romanovski. 2016. *Les réseaux de migrants haïtiano-guyanais dans l'espace américain*. Paris: L'Harmattan.

Zéphirin, Romanovski. 2017a. "The Politics and Policy Implications of Widespread Immigrations in French Guyana." In *Migrants: Public Attitudes, Challenges and Policy Implications*, edited by Stuart Rodriquez: 59–110. New York: NOVA Science Publishers. Collection Immigration in the 21st Century: Political, Social and Economic Issues.

Zéphirin, Romanovski. 2017b. "Why Migrant Network and International Migration Cannot Be Schematically Separated?" In *Migrants: Public Attitudes, Challenges and Policy Implications*, edited by Stuart Rodriquez: 275–283. New York: NOVA Science Publishers. Collection Immigration in the 21st Century: Political, Social and Economic Issues.

Zéphirin, Romanovski. 2018. "The Americas' Multi-Polar Displacements as a New Pattern in Haitian-French-Guyanese Migrations." *International Migration Journal*—IOM. Available Online (01 June), https://doi.org/10.1111/imig.12470.

# 4

# Moving from the Significance of the Geopolitics and the Geo-sociology of Globalization in Latin America to a Theoretical Framework for Research

## Abstract

Decades of economic globalization pertain emigration, immigration, return migrations, urban-rural land use, and urban landscape change. The consequences impact politics and policy on various geographical scales, as immigrants don't cross only transnational borders of neighboring regional countries in the south of the continent, but also move north and often transit through central America and the Caribbean. The strategies of integration and/or reintegration cause changes in social structures, social stratifications, social classes, territorial transformation, and economic mutation affecting politics and policy on various geographical scales. All these are driving factors of the geo-sociology of globalization in Latin America. Globalization through its various integrated networks disarticulates, rearticulates, connects, and transcends scattered locations and places in Latin America.

In this perspective, theoretical approaches coined by Martin and Taylor (2001) and Bogue (2012) address migration management and economic globalization respectively in high-income migration countries in the north of the continent and low- and middle-income ones in its south.

Also, in complement to the abovementioned (and among others), Zéphirin (2005, 2016, 2017), in a migration space system account, federates and goes beyond key theoretical contributions from the inter-American migration system (Smith 2001), migrant network (Massey 1987), and international immigration network (Krissman 2005) to analyze complex, scattered, and transnational migrations within the Americas.

Consequently, building the geo-sociology of globalization in Latin America as a multidisciplinary research object and elaborating testable hypotheses require researchers to explore methodological and theoretical challenges in order to balance quantitative and qualitative inquiries and explain concrete strategies, routes, trajectories, activities, and practices of diverse migrants' networks on borderless territories.

Keywords: globalization, migration, cities, geo-sociology, geopolitics, the Americas, theoretical framework, research.

## Introduction

Free-trade areas do not automatically generate high income for all in the production chain. While intra Latin American migrations allow people to establish migrant networks and to move in international migrant network on a hierarchical system of spaces, they do not significantly spark upward mobility in comparison to the United States and Canada. How does one evaluate transnational migration in cities as a geo-sociology of globalization in Latin America, and how does one conduct migration and return migration research on borderless territories?

The interaction of theoretico-methodological and practical interfaces sheds light on the issue of migration in the geo-sociology of globalization.

1. *Shifting development paradigm, the raising of globalization and spatial consequences*

Migration and urbanization reflect a development[57] policy (Norton 2007, 69) shift in Latin America (Barton 2003). In the diverse mobility strategies of people, they create their own space-construction in new densely populated urban areas. The interactions of composite populations with different ethnic and socioeconomic backgrounds produced new socio-spatial and political tensions and conflicts while trying to achieve socioeconomic promotion in new urban and social structures.

Between individual socio-spatial itineraries from rural to urban areas and from national to transnational places of living of migrations and return migrations, strained relationships and perceptions of space, politics, and power change become obvious. Dealing with causes and effects of human movements and urban settlements ignites socio-spatial practices and the emergence of new political geographies. As a result, among other issues, migration, cities, and globalization stand out prominently as threefold in Latin American geopolitics.

Since the early 1970s, people migrated from rural areas to urban ones. Transformation of landownership patterns and rural economies, along with industrial labor demand, precipitated a transformation of urban spaces with urban sprawl in large cities. The rapid urban growth with large concentration of people without the necessary infrastructures and public services to accommodate them profoundly modified the urban landscape, marginalizing the urban poor in comparison to standard urban neighborhoods for the (well-off) more privileged in the society. The uneven urbanization at national

---

[57] The general meaning of this term involves measures of economic growth, social welfare, and modernization. In human geography, the term of development can be of real value in highlight spatial distribution in income well-being, but also in reference of variations in social and cultural considerations. Such variations are evident in the developed world, particularly in change through time, different areas, and landscape. Views of development can be different as we move from liberal to Marxist perspectives.

levels reverberates on population composition and distribution on urban spaces, raising the issues of urban environmental protection, vulnerabilities, and safe, healthy workplace environments in new sprawling urban areas. Moving from rural poor to urban poor causes social tensions, conflicts, and sociopolitical movements and changes while people try to adapt to new development programs and policies.

In many cases, migrations are consequential to development policy shift from import substitution to structural adjustment economic policies (Barton 2003, Ocampo and Martin 2003). This trend led export economy to participate in globalization and benefit from comparative advantage. Globalization and free trade allow capital, goods, and humans to flow and increase high profits in annual incomes by big firms and corporations from North, Central, and South America. In the frame of opportunities offered by globalization (Pulsipher 2015), people's movement, motives, and patterns impact their spatial distribution and settlements in many countries in Latin America. Globalization and development amplified the age of information technology (IT), free trade, and cheap labor and created an economic competition among neighboring countries, which forced them to adjust, in some ways, their educational capabilities to take advantage of them. The process generates consequences in terms of reorientation of employment, education training, knowledge intensive job, and impacts on cities' social structure, population composition, settlement pattern, and spatial production.

The new impact on urban migration manifested in the combination of factors, such as the local politics and policy structuration and restructuration of cities. It also affected the emergence of new urban socioeconomic and development policy in their federate interactions on various geographical scales to drive political geographies of contemporary urban centers and cities in Latin America and the Caribbean, which goes over a simple traditional lens of geopolitics, narrowly defined as political and military spheres of influence.

Additionally, the complex geographical trajectories and urban settlement strategies of migrants both from national displacements and from international movements in neighboring countries raise the issues, on the one hand, of integration of migrants in new cosmopolitan cities, and on the other hand, of illegal transnational bor-der-crossing and national security problems expressed in political dis-course and repulsive public attitudes. These in turn affect interstate relations and diplomacy to curb the flow of migrants moving from low- and middle-income countries in Latin America to higher eco-nomic brackets in the northern part of the continent. In other words, migration, cities, development, and globalization are encompassing factors highlighting a new sense of Latin American geopolitics.

Also, since the mid-1980s, market openness and integra-tion become a corollary element to economic growth and poverty reduction in the dominant world liberal economic framework. Paraphrasing Professor Arvind Panagariya of Columbia University, Anderson and Nash (2006, 123) state that

> although trade openness is not by itself suf-ficient to trigger growth, it is clearly necessary. Particularly the need for economic liberalization is felt in agriculture, largely first because the majority of employments in developing countries comes from agriculture or agricultural goods sec-ond, rural poverty outnumbers urban poverty.

However, trade openness and labor liberalization have their advocates and their opponents. In this view, arguments are compet-ing on the issues.

Briefly, those who favor market liberalization, free-trade zones, and globalization argue that

> comparative advantage in production increased (with trade) economies of scales (in production)…so that intra as well as inter-indus-try trade can flourish…, trade barriers allowed imperfect competition to prevail in the domes-tic marketplace, avoid redundant knowledge creation through openness…, open economies tend to attract more investment from abroad,

> while raise the stock capital. (Anderson and Nash
> 2006, 128)

However, those who oppose the market openness "see trade reform as contributing to world economic dominance by multilateral firms, and certain unpleasant aspects of globalization, as inflicting grievous social and environmental ills in rich and poor countries alike" (Anderson and Nash 2006, 128).

In this perspective of pros and cons in argumentations about globalization and free-trade areas, three competing positions emerge. First, some support a full-trade liberalization. They defend that developing countries would gain disproportionately. Benefits could be great from south-south as from south-north trade reform. Agriculture is where liberalization is needed most. By far the greatest cuts in bound tariffs and subsidies are required in agriculture. Second,

> some countries expect to gain from partial
> liberalization, while they legally bound domestic from support commitments and agricultural
> tariffs, apply rates of protection and do subsidies, sensitive products receive lesser cuts...in
> their most protected goods, lowering barriers to
> imports of nonagricultural goods and services...
> [to] help balance the exchange of concessions
> between them and the developed countries...
> [they] reform their own trade policies. (Anderson
> and Nash 2006, 136)

While the first and the second tendencies in globalization and free-trade areas promote to remove totally and partially trade barriers, a third conception simply advocates to retain protectionist policies. As a matter of fact,

> the most compelling explanation for the
> persistence of trade barriers is based on politi-

cal economy. The changes in product prices that
result from trade liberalization or cuts in subsidies necessarily change the prices for the services
of productive factors: land, labor and capital.
(Anderson and Nash 2006, 128)

Supporters of protectionist policies are among some nongov-
ernmental organizations (NGO) and internationalist sociopolitical
activists who oppose to globalization and trade liberalization and
World Trade Organization (WTO).

By the way, market openness policy in the economic globalization-migration, which is a component of this broader paradigm, also
has its pros and its cons.

Migration contents benefits and costs both for sending and
receiving countries (Goldin 2006). Many countries enjoy the benefits but oppose to the costs, and most of the repulsive attitudes come
up when it comes for a nation to deal with the costs of immigration
(Zéphirin 2017a). This kind of irrational anti-immigrant sentiment
impedes comprehensible immigration policy and interstate cooperation on managing transnational immigration linked to economic
globalization and labor market liberalization.

For instance, in terms of benefits for a sending country, it appears
that (among others) remittances help not only families and friends in
the origin country, but also the national trade balance of the country. These funds contribute to mitigate socioeconomic inequality
and reduce sociopolitical unrests in countries with low-employment
rates. In many cases, migrants' remittances outclass direct foreign
investments and foreign aid (Goldin 2006, Zéphirin 2014).

Also, in terms of costs, the origin countries of migrants often
lose a segment of their young and educated population. Sending
countries called that (simplistically) brain drain migration. But benefits and costs of migration for a sending country are multiple and
debatable.

Additionally, benefits and costs of migration don't concern only
sending countries but also receiving ones. In terms of benefits for
receiving countries (among others), for example, low-cost immigrant

labors can lower production costs, encouraging new domestic business formation (Goldin 2006). In terms of costs for the receiving countries, some native-born citizens, because of the low price of labor migrants, withdraw from the labor market and increase the unemployment rate. This is a common critique waved often against migrants, which is not totally proven in many cases. Because the job market is more complex than this biased economic perception, which unfortunately nurtures anti-immigrant sentiments and xenophobic reactions in countries receiving migrants.

In some measures, globalization and migration come up with the seamy side of free-trade areas and labor market liberalization through repulsive public attitudes toward immigrants. As a result, while economic globalization creates prosperity, allowing people around the world to tap into larger markets and benefit from high incomes and good life, "economic integration poses serious inherent risks... The globalization of trade and labor markets concerns about the effects of free trade on jobs and working conditions led to violent protests" (Bhargava 2006, 4). This is the reason why, while rejecting the alarmist view of globalization and market liberalization, the authors (of a chapter in this edited volume) strongly support the position stipulating that "any proposed trade agreement should undergo a careful empirical analysis of the likely net gains" (Anderson and Nash 2006, 132) because social, economic, political, and spatial consequences can be considerable to economic prosperity, social peace, and politico-institutional stability if poverty, inequality, and discrimination are not tackled.

2. *Intra-Latin American migrations, socioeconomic diversity in cities as urban governance*

Free market and labor market liberalization allow investors, producers, and workers to interact on spaces to produce goods. However, if the owners of means of production and managers enjoy the economic growth and high salaries, an important segment of the labor force living in low-paid jobs does not have the same way of living in cities. As a result, different socioeconomic conditions affect urban spaces in free-trade areas. The ethnic, socioeconomic, and demographic diversities of the urban population challenge traditional urban structures, which were often unprepared to accommodate high and rapid growth in population density.

In this view, while the housing market in many of these countries focused on the segment of the population with proper income to buy and rent standard houses, a large sector of the population involved in the good export production for the global economy struggles to live in decent houses. In consequence, the working class often looks for cheap dwellings located in nonurbanized or agricultural land in cities outskirts. In its causes and effects, low-income workers and their urban settlement practices blow out traditional urban structures and provoke sprawling often, which grows faster than local-municipal urban policy planning capacity.

The urban sprawling, when it is not well controlled by local authorities, is a driver of vulnerability, risk, and disaster, largely affecting the disadvantaged who often face flooding, landslides, etc. Uncontrolled urbanization and territorial exclusion in the margin of the regular city grid linked to the search for urban economic opportunities by the migrant workers and the working class at large are detrimental for environmental sustainability and inclusive development. The constitution of marginalized urban peripheral neighborhoods, very often, occurs without any harmonization of human and natural systems.

The uneven urban development characterizing many cities in Latin America often reverberates on poverty and inequality in socioeconomic conditions, which federate on space to show double-standard cities. In fact, formally designed on the one hand and informally built on the other hand characterize cities that coexist and embody profound social and inequality on spaces, paradoxically presenting high rates of economic growth. Sectoral urbanistic and exclusivist approaches by drawing and building zoning for the well-off are very limited in scopes and scales to encircle the systemic dimension of the spatial disparity in development.

Controlling urbanization (Chaleard 2014) in developing countries opened up for free-trade zones and labor market liberalization challenges local governments' public policy efficiency. In this view, poles and axes of growth in the urban explosion phenomenon often move at a faster pace than the local institutional response (Zéphirin 2005). Traditional urban extension plans, isolated urban zonings, or gated city projects, while they satisfy the demand for classy urban housing in protected and clean urban neighborhoods for the class of investors and managers of globalization, will not be enough to produce the city as a coherent and interacting system, which is definitely more than simple juxtaposition and unconnected urban segment or urbanized spots.

That is the challenge that the territories affected by free-trade zones and liberalization of labor markets have to overcome, risks (Bhargava 2006) of social unrest and anti-globalization protests in a perspective of deepening free-trade economic policy (Anderson and Nash 2006) to achieve human development goals.

In this matter, urban development and planning becomes an important part of poverty and inequality reduction for many in terms of urban governance, social cohesion, and human rights. Urban design, policy planning, and urban projects become a local socio-technic and political process where every actor sharing and producing the urban space is involved and wants to negotiate and finds a common ground to order, reorder, and make sense of urban territories as an artifact reflecting an attempt to include a diversity of interests intersecting on space.

Democratic and good governance and efficient public institutions are facing the challenge to tackle problems generated by the economic globalization. Building cities (Merlin 1991, Dupuis 1998, Choais 2014) through urban projects (Pinson 2000, Hayot and Sauvage 2000) raises the question for whom and with whom. These are key interrogations that urbanists, urban planners, geographers, architects, civil engineers, politicians, and elected officials, among others, are facing in dealing with urban governance and regeneration as a means of fixing the seamy side of market liberalization in developing countries. This also includes designing and implementing efficient urban and housing public policy in a multiethnic environment with diversity in socioeconomic conditions and discrepancy in citizens' rationales regarding spatial settlements.

For instance, some former migrant workers becoming new citizens opt for integration in their new homeland and affirm their socioeconomic "success" through single private family houses. In contrast, there are others who consider their dwellings in their host country as a temporary home and are waiting to move back home after a certain period of time. All these personal and collective behaviors contribute to changes in urban landscapes, urban structures, and urban forms through time (Zéphirin and Piantoni 2008).

Paradoxically, a deep understanding of these socio-spatial rationalities is keen to build up local-regional sociopolitical momentum for effective incremental housing public policy in a perspective of urban integration for a recomposed population spatially redistributed. More importantly, in a context of promoting the state official values of national integration and antidiscrimination policy, a clear understanding of untold socio-spatial settlement logics matters not only to design public housing as a means of advocating for poverty and inequality reduction policy, inclusion, and better interethnic relations in urban housing.

Through time, immigration policy will shift to migrant policy (Weiner 1995, Domenach 1995); once a stock of immigrants is spatially established and starting its absorption, both the social structure and the population structure will be affected. As a result, the different causes and effects of the population recomposition will be federated and reverberated on diverse geographical scales and ultimately drive new elements for territorial formation and territoriality.

3.   *Globalization, migration, and return migration in cities as political geography*

Paradoxically, market liberalization economic policy is generally led by right-wing politicians who largely support full removal of economic barriers and show reluctance to invest in social and human programs for those left behind by the pervasive effects of globalization. Now major multilateral international bodies of the global governance impel these rightist governments to commit to poverty reduction and inequality policy in order to mitigate sociopolitical and institutional instability.

Trade liberalization and economic integration go over ideological orthodoxy to build political consensus across the lines as a means of good democratic governance. Economic globalization purposes in Latin America in the post-Cold War era (Malawer 1998, Ocampo and Martin 2003) to promote democracy and peaceful resolution of conflicts in national political systems as a condition to create wealth and prosperity. However, from simple institutional democratic principles, many antiglobalization activists and left-wing organizations find in institutional democracy an opportunity to push for more democratization (Malawer 1998, Stark and Jeffrey 1994). Probably, democratization as a process is better suited to give a fair share to those who participate in high economic growth and wealth.

Aside from economic prosperity and those who are in the higher-class position, hierarchies in the social stratification, and those enjoying high incomes and the good life in free-trade zone areas, many of the disadvantaged are facing daily and structural problems of social class and racial discrimination in employment, inadequate housing, poverty, low-wage jobs, low incomes, and high unemployment rate. Women conditions in part-time jobs, promotion, and occupational advancement matter as social and gender issues in the labor market liberalization. In one way or the other, class relations and social and economic problems are connected to the class structure. The globalization, by allowing a free circulation of knowledge and a high-tech middle class to manage services in many cities in the Americas, facilitates upward socioeconomic mobility for many who will contribute in some degree to modify class hierarchies, class location, and interethnic relations.

In one way or the other, the space is where the abovementioned contradictions will be federated. And it will belong to elected officials to deal with them in a way to ease interactions and interrelations in social bodies, which are transcended by a geo-sociology of transnationality. The diversity of problems facing Latin American cities (Chaleard 2014, Brenner and Theodore 2005) consequential to market openness and labor market liberalization requires an increase in democratization of local political systems and their ability to build a political bridge to tackle common local-regional and transnational issues.

As a result, under conditions of political consensus over public policy agenda, design, and implementation (Muller and Surel 1998), it becomes obvious that either authoritarian urbanism or patronal urbanism (Merlin 1991) alone cannot solve the complexity of current urban social problems consequential to economic liberalization and integration. Going over exclusivist and sectoral approaches to build or manage the city will allow one to explore a broader perspective of urban governance, which becomes inevitable under current circumstances. In other words, urbanism between utopias and realities (Choais 2014) offers a physical and a multidisciplinary framework to deal with governance and governability of network transnational territories torn by a diversity of actors, interests, loci, and links (Zéphirin 2016). This complexity in territories shapes political geography of Latin American nations through new practices of locations, spaces, and places. Emigration, immigration, return migration, and migrants in different manners impact demographic, social, economic, and spatial structures in the Americas.

Efficient governance of transnationalized territories and their new social geography intersects with the principle of good democratic governance advocated by globalization's proponents (Anderson and Nash 2006), consolidation, and extension in Latin America.

Furthermore, in addressing the globalization issue, while siding with the core of Saskia Sassen's (1991, 1998) and William Robinson's (2012) works arguing transnational immigration in cities from low-income countries to high-income ones is one of the pendant of the global economy (alongside transnational investment capital, capital mobility, and global cities), the book's argumentations go further to underline some uncovered problematic elements in the nexus of globalization, transnational migration, and cities.

The abovementioned mainstream researchers focus mainly on one dimension of transnational people movements (i.e., immigration and quasi neglect of the return migrations as both are an autonomous aspect of the migration project and a spatial production driver).

The interplay of economic regionalization and transnational migrations reveals a great interconnection between immigration influxes, immigrant communities, and reversible migration tendencies in both global cities and newly regionalized free-trade zones in the Americas and their international network cities.

Aside from determinants of labor market division and structuration, immigrants and return migrants in cities experiencing regionalized-globalized economies in the Americas are also torn by voluntary integration and reintegration logics in urban structures.

Transnational investment capital, which drives immigration in the Americas' main regional international network cities and global cities, contributes to create an important "popular" informal capital mobility through remittances, causing a geo-social transnational territoriality with the reemergence of some decayed cities or some disrupted rural communities in peripheral developing countries.

Globalization cannot be based solely on transnational immigration to fully explain social geography and urban structuration in cities without systemically connecting it with reversible migration logics.

Countries' free-trade agreements and transnational people movements in South and Middle America's international network cities linked to global cities in northern America set the stage for reframing the inter-American migration space as an interacting and interconnecting system.

People movements connect local-national urban scale problems with migrations and immigration policies caused by globalization of regional economies, where interstate cooperation tries to cope with transnational contemporary issues as both interrelated factors and drivers of political geographies, geopolitics, and international relations in Latin America and the Caribbean, which, by the way, goes over a simple traditional lens of geopolitics, narrowly defined as political spheres of influence and military alliances.

Consequently, the findings provide credible facts and pertinent analytical perspectives to scholars in order to understand the complex interrelated factors that migration, cities, development, economic regionalization, globalization, and geopolitics stand out, interconnecting Latin American countries.

A multidisciplinary perspective deals with the complexity of Latin American development programs and policy consequentialness. These are prompted by urban migrations, city management, and sociopolitical processes of production of space for socioeconomic actors with different rationales who live, work, and circulate in multicultural cities. At the same time, they are also connecting local-national urban scale problems with migrants and immigration policies caused by globalization of regional economies, where interstate cooperation tries to cope with transnational contemporary issues as both interrelated factors and drivers of political geographies, geopolitics, and international relations.

However, the book does not frame geopolitics through a traditional theoretical framework of strategic dimensions of border and territorial disputes, spheres of political influence, and military alliances to protect vital economic interests, but through a new lens of peoples' concrete practices of places and politics. The spatial analysis intersects geopolitics. Consequently, the book thematically refers to academic disciplines such as economy, sociology, demography, human geography, political geography, regional geography, urban geography, urbanism, political science, international relations, and development studies.

4.  *Doing research: practical and theoretical implications of the geo-sociology of globalization*

As wrote Norton (2007, 74), a human geographer, globalization breaks and connects basic and traditional "geographic concepts of location, space and place and transforms them in a mega-concept." Building a multidisciplinary research object on scattered transnational loci where people live, circulate, and work poses the problem of criticizing past knowledge or existing of a priori knowledge (Casullo 2005) to explore new empirical grounded evidences and experiences. In this view, the constitution of market liberalization and job market deregulation, allowing a transnational workforce to move and/or settle in different places through various types of migrations (Goldin 2006), raises the question of transforming new experiences in new knowledge in order to highlight new problems in regional transnational people movements.

In many ways, this is an epistemic move to consider in terms of critical philosophical reflection and a theory of knowledge on traditional accounts and research methods (quantitative and qualitative) to deal with transnational migrations on interconnected neighboring countries with migrants' networks crossed by international migration networks (Massey 1987; Krissman 2005; Zéphirin 2005, 2016).

Revising conditions in which researchers and scholars come up with premises in cogent arguments matter to justify existing theoretical accounts in migration studies or defy current research perspectives by going over the existence of a priori knowledge defined by Albert Casullo (2005, 42) as "independent of experience" in reference to John Stuart Mills.

Epistemology of knowledge as a philosophy of knowledge on the practice of doing research requires to shift from some outdated knowledge when they become beliefs to allow new experiments from new practices and new problematic constructions in order to emerge innovative knowledge and theoretical perspectives. As a result, doing innovative research on many transnational loci with multinational distributed population and their diverse practices regarding sociality and habitability raises the question on how to collect and produce relevant data from a seasonal, fluctuating, and often "invisible" or "underground" population who look for better economic opportunities in free economic zones with attractive immigrant workplace policy.

The enlargement of territories by transnational activities not only by global investor elites, but also by a transnational workforce, stand out social and economic practices, which, while being spatially localized in a host country, its cities develop autonomous strategies on urban-rural lands through variable and reversible influxes of people involved in integration and/or reintegration. These new conditions of migration in cities and their territories involved in the economic globalization and integrative structures impel scholars who do research.

Once again, there is a preoccupation about not only the cogency of premises, theses, arguments, survey production, and its balance on many loci in order to find the population where it is precisely and timely located as a means of scientific observation, analysis, representativity, relevance, and pertinence to question the permanence or not of methods and theories in an attempt to highlight the varying and flexible nature of transnational and scattered migrations on multipolar loci in the Americas (Zéphirin 2005, 2016).

The complex factors involved in transnational migrations in Latin America go over a single discipline to reach a multidisciplinary perspective that shapes this book. Among other approaches, socio-economic, geopolitical, legal, spatial, and demo-social contribute in the theoretical corpus explaining the transnational dimension of the migrations and in their different causes and effects. As a result and under some circumstances, some theoretical accounts are prioritized to the detriment of others.

Consequently, migrant network (Massey 1987) associates push (emigration) and pull (immigration) factors to explain people movements from developing countries to developed ones in a search for external job opportunities in more prosperous economies. Once arrived in their host countries, immigrants connected to their origin country (and rural villages) allow others to continue to come and enlarge their network. This theory portrays very well the constitution of pioneers on the short term.

However, in the long term, it shows some limitations to explain some complex factors and a variety of actors involved in the continuity of migration flows. This is the reason why Krissman's (2005) work criticizing Massey's migrant network theory is relevant. As an alternative, Krissman (2005) proposed to shift from migrant network to international migrant network in order to encompass the diversity of factors and the variety of actors left out by Massey (1987). However, if Krissman (2005) underlines a crucial point, he also failed in regard to many parameters to seize broader dimensions of the migrant network theoretical problems.

Krissman (2005) attempted to mechanically separate migrant networks from international migration networks (Zéphirin 2005, 2016), which, more importantly, does not use the autonomous return migrations and the diversity of geographical spaces and actors involved in international migrations to bridge the theoretical gap between the two currents. As a result, Zéphirin (2017b) connects migrant networks and international migrant networks as both sides in the same coin to explain transnational people movements on various hierarchical geographical scales, theoretically conceptualized as an interacting system of spaces for migrations. Also, immigrants' strategies of autonomous integration (in the host country) and/or reintegration (in the origin country) play an important role in connecting the two theoretical perspectives with the empirical evidences of transnational migrations in the Americas.

Moreover, in regard to globalization migration, Martin and Taylor (2001) rightly outline the fact that free-trade agreements between developed and developing countries will continue in the short term to increase migrants' entry in developed countries because of wage disparity. Only in the long term and with a decrease in salary gap will migration from developing to developed countries significantly be reduced.

However, if this theory is relevant in many regards, it shows some limitations to overemphasize receiving developed countries and neglect, at some point, developing ones in the migration equation. Because the network of "central command cities" described by Sassen Saskia (1991) as one of the key mechanisms of the globalization connects not only developed countries' cities and developing countries' ones, but also intersects south-south cities and their migrations.

In this view, Donald Bogue's (2012) findings fill the theoretical gap between south-north migrations studies and bring some fresh thinking in south-south or intra Latin American migrations. He finds in his works that immigration among Latin American countries fails to improve income. Bogue's (2012) study was based on three types of socio-professional profiles: "lower skilled people, intermediate skilled people, and people with specialized skills." In order to compare immigration between the United States and Latin America, he draws his conclusion, and Bogue (2012) collected and analyzed data on migrants' education level, employment status, and length of residency in twelve Latin American countries. His work contributes to clarify the intra Latin American migrations.

However, despite the importance of his findings, some precautions need to be taken about the rapid generalization of his conclusions because of diversity in migrants' conditions, the different geographical scales of provenance of migrants, the time of the start of the migration project, and ethnic and socio-professional profiles.

## Conclusion

Finally, the chapter shows that globalization in its different causes and effects and benefits and costs allows many to take advantage of wealth creation, economic growth, and good life. But also, others are struggling, particularly transnational undocumented migrants and low-skilled workers.

And all of the abovementioned theoretical accounts (among others) dealing with migration, cities, and globalization as Latin American geopolitics contribute to shed light on and answer central introductory questions of the book, focusing on how to evaluate the geo-sociology of the globalization.

And what is its theoretical underpinning? Particularly, aside from the diverse and complementary theoretical contributions used in this book, because of the complexity of transnational people movements transcending locations, spaces, and places, the book shares Bogue (2012) findings that intra Latin American migrations do not significantly generate upward mobility through increasing income. This is the reason why migrants accumulate migration experiences in different countries with various migrant networks and crossed by diverse international migration networks on a multipolar scattered system of spaces in looking for higher income. This rationale leads many Latin American migrants to move from the southern to the northern part of the American continent.

In this view, on a theoretical standpoint, by bridging the theoretical gap between migrant network and international migration network on a scattered and multipolar system of spaces (Zéphirin 2018), including Sassen's (1991) and Robinson's (2009) works on globalization and network cities, Zéphirin (2016) broadens his problematical field of research to integrate, at some point, useful complementary theoretical contributions from both Martin and Taylor (2001) and Bogue (2012). In other words, the book, while relying mainly on the core theoretical accounts of migrant network and international migration network on an interacting system of spaces for migration, usefully cooperates with other theories and findings to largely evaluate and explain the geo-sociology of globalization as complex transnational people movements in Latin American cities as a driver of geopolitics.

In this view, while the global city (Sassen 1991) theoretical framework emphasizing on the "decentralization of central command urban centers" of global investment capital and fragmentation of production in the globalization, the city diplomacy (Chan 2017) perspective points out, to some degree, not only the seamy side of the globalization on international urban systems, but also the multilateral diplomatic efforts to comprehensively and collaboratively fix its (the globalization) diverse human-made, multiscalar, and transnational disruptions.

The growing importance of Latin American cosmopolitan cities impels the research community, elected officials, political activists, etc., to pay attention to the city diplomacy paradigm as a means of sharing best local-regional policy practices and leadership experiences at a time when municipal governments and national states try to find a common ground on some key multilateral diplomatic agreements and global compacts (such as the UN sustainable development goals [SDG] and the climate multilateral accord) to implement them locally and nationally.

Exploring this type of local leadership in foreign policy through the city diplomacy perspective (alongside the national states' prerogatives of handling foreign relations) to both foster a long-term and a multiscalar common diplomatic understanding and govern global challenges would allow to mitigate, to some degree, local-regional discontents of the globalization (Stiglitz 2002) and adapt local-regional cities to the global environmental climate change and inclusive urban sustainable development. Definitely, designing a progressive research agenda on the geopolitics of globalization cannot be set without a city diplomacy approach in the Western Hemisphere at large.

Consequently, the traditional partnership among economic players from Latin American and North American regions was recently extended to the rising power of China in Southeast Asia, which entered the game through involvements in financing development infrastructures. This is a new element in the globalization equation that raises the need to put in perspective the subject, which, by the way, requires going beyond the integrative economic bodies connecting and interacting subregions in the Western Hemisphere in the post-Cold War era.

In that purpose, it becomes crucial to scholars to consider, apart from internal dynamic forces, how current regional transnational issues in the context of the emergence of China in the economic globalization, its global-regional political intentions, and the traditional regional partnership with the United States will determine the prospect of the Latin American future in dealing with migration, cities, development, and globalization as geopolitics.

# References

Anderson, Kym and John D. Nash. 2006. "Trade Reform and the Doha Development Agenda." In *Global Issues for Global Citizens. An Introduction to key Development Challenges* (edited by Vinay Bhargava): 123–143. Washington, DC: World Bank.

Bhargava, Vinay. 2006. "Introduction to Global Issues." In *Global Issues for Global Citizens. An Introduction to Key Development Challenges.* Edited by Vinay Bhargava:1–28. Washington, DC: World Bank.

Barton, Jonathan R. 2003. *A Political Geography of Latin America* (ebook). London: Taylor and Francis.

Bogue, Donald J. 2012. *The Economic Adjustment of Immigrants to twelve nations of Latin American and Comparison with United States.* Population Research Center and Center on Aging. Chicago: The University of Chicago.

Brenner, N. and N. Theodore. 2005. Neoliberalism and the Urban Condition. *City*, 9: 101–106. https://doi.org/10.1080/13604810500092106.

Casullo, Albert. 2005. "Epistemic Overdetermination and Priori Justification." In *Epistemology.* Edited by John Hawthorne, *Journal Philosophical Perspective* 19: 41–58.

Castle, Stephen and Mark J. Miller. 2009. *The Age of Migration: International Population Movements in the Modern World.* New York: Palgrave Macmillan.

Chaléard, Jean-Louis, ed. 2014. *Métropoles aux Suds, le Défi des Périphéries*, Paris: Karthala.

Chan, Dan Koon-hong. 2017. "City Diplomacy and 'Glocal' Governance: Revitalizing Cosmopolitan Democracy." *European Planning Studies Journal* 10, no. 15.

Choais, Francoise. 2014. *Urbanisme, Utopies et Réalités.* Paris: Seuil.

Domenach, Hervé and Michel Picouet. 2004. *Population, Environnement et Développement. La Durabilité en Question.* Paris: L'Harmattan.

Di Meo, Guy. 1998. *Géographie sociale et territoire.* Paris: Nathan Université.

Dupuis, Gabriel. 1991. *L'urbanisme des réseaux—Théories et méthodes.* Paris: Armand Colin.

Goldin, Ian. 2006. "Globalizing with their Feet: The Opportunities and Costs of International Migration." In *Global Issues for Global Citizens. An Introduction to Key Development Challenges.* Edited by. Vinay Bhargava: 105–121. Washington, DC: World Bank.

Hayot, D'Alain and André Sauvage. 2000. *Le projet urbain. Enjeux, expérimentations et professions.* Paris: Editions de la Villette.

Krissman, Fred. 2005. "Sin Coyote Ni Patron: Why the Migrant Network Fails to Explain International Migration." *International Migration Review (IMR)*, vol. 39. no.1. (spring): 4–44.

Lehman, David. 1990. *Democracy and Development in Latin America. Economics, Politics, and Religion in the post-War Period.* Philadelphia: Temple University Press.

Malawer, Stuart S. 1988. "The Political Economy of International Relations by Robert Gilpin," In *Maryland Journal of International Law,* vol.12, issue 2, article 6: 307–311.

Merlin, Pierre. 1991. *L'Urbanisme.* Paris: Que Sais-Je? PUF.

Muller, Pierre and Yves Surel. 1998. *L'Analyse des politiques publiques.* Paris: Monchrestien.

Martin, Philip L. and Edward J. Taylor. 2001. "Managing Migration: The Role of Economic Policies": 95–120. In Aristide Zolberg and Peter M. Benda, *Global Migrants Global Refugees. Problems and Solutions.* New York: Berghahn Books.

Massey, S. Douglas et al. 1987. *Return to Aztlan: The Social Process of International Migration from Western Mexico.* Berkeley: University of California.

Massey, Douglas. 1993. "Theories of International Migration," *Population and Development Review,* 19 (3).

Norton, William. 2007. *Human Geography* Sixth Edition. New York: Oxford University Press.

Ocampo, Jose Antonio and Juan Martin. 2003. *Globalization and Development. A Latin American and Caribbean Perspective.* Santiago, Chile: ECLAC.

Pulsipher, Lydia Mihelic and Alex Pulsipher. 2015. *World Regional Geography Concepts* (Third Edition). W. H. Freeman and Company. New York: Macmillan Education Company.

Robinson, William I. 2009. "Sassen Saskia and The Sociology of Globalization—A Critical Appraisal." In *Sociological Analysis* 1, no. 3 (Spring):5–30.

Sassen, Saskia. 1991. *The Global City: New York, London, Tokyo.* Princeton: Princeton University Press.

Sassen, Saskia. 1998. *The Mobility of Capital and Labor: A Study in International Investment and Labor Flow.* Cambridge: Cambridge University Press.

Sassen, Saskia. 2007. *A Sociology of Globalization.* New York: W. W. Norton.

Smith, C. Robert. 2001. "Current Dilemmas and Future Prospects of the Inter-American Migration System," in A. R. Zolberg and P. M. Benda, eds. *Global Migrants Global Refugees. Problems and Solutions*: 121–167. New York: Berghahn Books.

Stark, Jeffrey. 1998. "Globalization and Democracy in Latin America," In *Fault Lines of Democracy in Post-Transition Latin America*: 67–96. Edited by Felipe Aguero and Jeffrey Stark. Miami: North-South Center Press at the University of Miami.

Stiglitz, Joseph S. 2002. *Globalization and its Discontents.* New York and London: W. W. Norton and Company.

Weiner, Myron. 1995. *The Global Migration Crisis. Challenge to States and to Human Rights.* New York: Harper Collins.

Weiner, Myron and Michael S. Teitelbaum. 2001. *Political Demography—Demographic Engineering.* New York: Berghahn Books.

Zéphirin, Romanovski. 2005. *Le Champ migratoire haïtiano-guyanais: étude des causes et effets politiques, socio-économiques et spatiaux. Multipolarité et réversibilité dans le système migratoire interaméricain.* Aix-en-Provence: Thèse de Doctorat sous la direction de Hervé Domenach, Université Aix-Marseille III, Faculté de Droit, d'Economie et des Sciences-IUAR (Institut d'Urbanisme et d'Aménagement Régional).

Zéphirin, Romanovski. 2017a. "The Politics and Policy Implications of Widespread Immigrations in French Guyana." In *Migrants: Public Attitudes, Challenges and Policy Implications* (edited by Stuart Rodriquez): 59–110. New York: NOVA Science Publishers. Collection Immigration in the 21st Century: Political, Social and Economic Issues.

Zéphirin, Romanovski. 2017b. "Why Migrant Network and International Migration Cannot Be Schematically Separated?" In *Migrants: Public Attitudes, Challenges and Policy Implications*, edited by Stuart Rodriquez: 275–283. New York: NOVA Science Publishers. Collection Immigration in the 21st Century: Political, Social and Economic Issues.

Zéphirin, Romanovski. 2018. "The Americas' Multi-Polar Displacements as a New Pattern in Haitian-French-Guyanese Migrations." *International Migration Journal*—IOM (01 June). Available Online, https://doi.org/10.1111/imig.12470.

# 5

# Conclusion: Merging Geopolitics and Globalization Theories; Implications for Migration and Cities

## Abstract

From the political and security strategies of the containment against communism during the 1970s and the mid-1980s, to the liberal free trade and economic integration model from the end of the 1980s to date, the region of the Americas has changed and produced a new political geography and geopolitics. The combined diverse integrated flows within the globalization and the quasi general adoption of institutional democracy pave the way for the emergence of two new dimensions of political geography and geopolitics in the Americas.

First, the capitalist logic of territorial expansion and its liberal control over neighboring countries through economic liberalization and integration put forth the liberal democracy and influence groupings of states' domestic and foreign policies in the region.

Second, among other diverse flows, human mobility, migration and spatial settlements-resettlements, urban relocation practices in cities and rural areas in the inter-American region spark some specific practices, perception, and representations of spaces and places. Human mobility on diverse geographical scales differently displays the economic regionalization-globalization of the Western Hemisphere.

Consequently, both dimensions in their opposition and their complementarity, in their diverse interconnected causes and effects, shape the political geography and geopolitics in the Americas. This is the reason why studying the geopolitics of globalization matters to figure out the interplay of the economical and the political over people movements and migrations in network cities and urban governance in the regionalized Americas.

Keywords: regionalization, globalization, political geography, geopolitics, migration, cities, world systems, social constructivism, and deconstructivism.

## Shifting Drivers in Americas' Geopolitics

The region and the regionalization of the Americas are intertwined with population movements and human settlements in spaces and places in the past centuries (Barton 2003, Mercille 2008, Mamaadouh and Muller 2017).

European colonizers brought by force with them in the Americas people from Africa (largely), Asia, and the Pacific (to a lesser extent) to settle colonies. Rivalries among great European colonial powers played a key role, not only in bringing an amount of imported population to (largely) replace the decimated native American Indians by a composite immigrant population, but also by creating a pattern of human and spatial settlements.

The pattern of land occupation corresponded to some particular patterns of economic production, social structure, and strategic military defense of colonial territories crossing all over the Americas. In this view, plantation colonies and settlement colonies, both in their opposition and their complement, contributed to create a particular colonial political geography and geopolitics in the Americas from the fifteenth to the nineteenth centuries. However, the rise of anti-colonialist, anti-slavery, and independent movements across the Americas in the early nineteenth century broke away from this old colonial political geography and geopolitics to pave the way for a new independent and nationalist perception and representation of space, people, politics, power, and state interactions in the Americas. This is in itself a big shift in political geography and geopolitics in the Western Hemisphere.

In this perspective, during the early nineteenth century, the twentieth century, and until now in the early twenty-first century, the emergence of the United States of America as the dominant regional power firstly, and as a world superpower, replaced the European style of political geography and modified the old geopolitics.

The use of the Monroe Doctrine, summarized by the phrase "America for the Americans," played an important role to keep the colonialists Europeans off the Americas and, paradoxically, to establish a new era of the United States dominance called imperialism by Central America, the Caribbean, and South America (Portes and Grosfoguel 1994, Knight 1990, Hillman and D'Agostino 2003).

In this view, the newly coined concept of Latin America, by opposition to the North American dominance, marked the resentment or the unwillingness of some parts of the Americas to accept the economic, sociocultural, political, and military expansion of the United States in new independent states' territories in the Western Hemisphere region (Manigat 1991).

The new geopolitics of the United States moving roughly from anticolonialism to imperialism and anticommunism considerably shaped people movements, human settlements, spaces, places, politics, power, and security forces in the Americas.

Large-scale human migrations in the Americas, particularly Central America and the Caribbean, started (aside from the old colonial European era) with the penetration of big North American food companies and their investments. The new investments looking for a cheap labor force sparked inter-American migrations that interact and merge people from Puerto Rico, Cuba, Haiti, Jamaica, the Dominican Republic, Panama, etc. (Portes and Grosfoguel 1994).

Historically, the geopolitics of the United States's capitalist expansion in Latin American territories started with the investments of the big farming companies (in sugar and banana production, among others), causing in the nineteenth and twentieth centuries waves of inter-American migrations.

This is the historical and human context for the foundation of the inter-American migration system (Smith 2001) and the multipolar migration system (Zéphirin 2005, 2016, 2018).

Aside from the economic dimension of inter-American migrations connected to the economic aspect of US geopolitics (Mitchell 1994, Forsythe et al. 2001), the containment strategy to fight the communist expansion in the Americas, in its diverse causes and effects, allowed displaced populations and migrations on various geographical scales to settle or resettle in different spaces and places across the Americas (in the second half of the twentieth century). People movements caused by economic, political, and security factors are also a dimension in political geography and geopolitics in the Americas. As a result, the liberal geoeconomics framed itself as the dominant geopolitical driver shaping politics and policy in the region.

Since the end of the nineteenth century and the entire twentieth century, the end of colonialism in the Americas and the emergence of the United States as a great regional, world, and global power and a dominant economic and political entity shaped economic production, security forces, political powers, and, to some extent, the territorial organizations and the socio-spatial structures through human mobilities and patterns of human settlements in many inter-American countries directly or indirectly (influenced by the United States's economic and security interactions in terms of space, politics, and power relations).

However, since the end of the Cold War in 1991 and the beginning of the twenty-first century and the post-Cold War, without any fundamental but tactical contradiction, the rise of economic liberalization and regional integration confirms the predominance of geo-economics[58] (as the new form) over "past forms" of geopolitics in the Americas (Sparke 2014, 12).

---

[58] Sparke (2014), in analyzing the ties between the US hegemony and the market hegemony globally, refers to many authors and writes that

> According to to Perry Anderson, such economic dominance when combined with America's military

The preeminence of geoeconomics[59] over the traditional geo-politics plays an important role in the institutional democracy and political freedom in the Americas. As a new driving force for insti-tutional democracy and post-Cold War geopolitics, geoeconomics combines state and nonstate actors in designing and implementing states' foreign policy. Geoeconomics becomes dominant and under-mines the traditional political and security drivers in geopolitics in the Americas. To some extent, the overshadowing of the former Cold War geopolitics by the post-Cold War geoeconomics relates to the economic regionalization-globalization in the Americas.

However, the geoeconomics' predominance in shaping space-power relations in geopolitics and international relations does not go without problems. As a matter of fact, new regional-national issues generated by the geoeconomics' consequentialness in the regionaliza-tion-globalization of the economies of the Americas create the diverse conditions and go over geoeconomics and the globalization frame-work to reach more regional-global issues, sparking local, regional, national, and global issues; asking for collective cooperation; redefin-ing space, power, and space time.

---

dominance (and underpinned, he also argues in a rather too environmentally determinist flourish, by America's physical geography) allows the USA to swing away from a hegemony of consent towards a hegemony of force. (Anderson, 2002)

Adopting a more political geographical (as opposed to a physical geographical) approach, Leo Panitch and Sam Gindin (2003) argue that America's long success in extending a hegemony of consent around liberal capitalism has now come face to face with its limits in the periphery. The result, they suggest, is a geographical division of hegemony with ongoing hegemonies of consent in the core and scattered hegemonies of dominance in the periphery as nonperforming, nondisciplining states are brought back into line. (Sparke 2014, 12).

[59] "The governance of international borders has shown how the border-softening emphasis in flat-world business discourse…geoeconomics…shapes both national and transnational statecraft" (Sparke 2014, 26–27).

The dominance of geoeconomics over old forms of geopolitics bridges the gap between globalization and global-regional-local issues.

Consequently, the geoeconomics, in its diverse causes and effects in terms of transnational migration-remigration, urban mobility and settlement patterns, urban poverty and inequality reduction policy (Zéphirin 2020), inter-ethnic relations, political participation, and the claim of well-being and human rights becomes a matter of political geography, critical geopolitics, and radical geopolitics.

In other words, the old form of Cold War geopolitics in the Americas is significantly replaced by a new one in the post-Cold War era dominated by geoeconomics[60] (in both critical geopolitics and

---

[60] If Sparke (2014) portrayed geoeconomics as the reflection of the "combined United States economic and military dominance as first a hegemony of consent, and second a hegemony of force crossing both the core and the periphery through the globalized economy," for his part, Julien Mercille (2008), simply portrays *geoeconomics* as the outmatch of politics in the geopolitics of globalization in the context of the post-Cold War era. While Sparke (2014) is very cautious to compare the current "geoeconomics" (in the age of globalization as a new form of geopolitics) with the past form of geopolitics of the Cold War, Mercille (2008) clearly takes this step to associate the liberal transnational "geoeconomics" as an expression of the political geography and geopolitics of the post-Cold War.

Once again, Sparke (2014, 10, 11) lays out the problematic foundations (above, as mental map of the global political economy) to explain his conceptual move from Luttwak's (1993) restrictive view of "geoeconomics," but he is very hesitant, contrary to Mercille (2008), to rise "geoeconomics" as the new form of geopolitics of the post-Cold War and the globalization. In other words, it is important to note that not only Julien Mercille (2008) underlines the fact that "geoeconomics" outpaces traditional political and security parameters in the new form of the geopolitics of the globalization, more importantly, he clearly stated that he focuses on observing and analyzing the "balance, the tensions and the conflict between them, with the dominant role of 'geoeconomics' to the detriment of old political and security drivers" of geopolitics within the globalization.

Because for Mercille (2008), while "geoeconomics" is dominant with the globalization as a matter of geopolitics, it has not a fundamental contradiction with the "politics and security" drivers. Their contradiction is simply tactical within the capitalist globalization. As a matter of fact, analyzing key issues such as peace, war, security, economic prosperity, and progress within the globalization

radical geopolitics), which is heavily impacted by diverse regional-global flows as a matter of political geography and geopolitics.

The economic regionalization of the Americas is rooted in a broader globalization process, which has diverse consequences.

In this view, globalization contextualized in the post-Cold War has significantly evolved. By the end of the 1990s and roughly after two decades (2000–2010 and 2010–2020), globalization was mainly focused on representation in terms of people representation and institutionalized control of global economic forces. Particularly, the World Trade Organization (WTO) was targeted by some who are opposed to the global hegemonic economic actors and major world leaders leading globalization (Sparke 2014).

In this view, the global networks and flows identifying globalization are seriously questioned by grassroots and unions in terms of political implications for national states and the worldwide working-class and precarious people in general. The international political consequences of market-led globalization are the adoption by some major international organizations and of some multilateral accords on the global environmental and sustainable development such as the Kyoto Protocol (and many more), addressing environmental and the climate challenges as a matter of global governance.

Supporters and opponents of market-driven globalization fall apart over some key questions such as national security and sovereignty of nation states within the economic regionalization-integration process. According to Sparke (2014, 10), "The neoliberalization of geopolitics" is consequential to "borderless...nation states" experiencing globalization, which is called *globalist geoeconomic*. The political ideological discourse over globalization has its pros and cons. While the pros of globalization present it as unstoppable and

---

becomes crucial to understand the first (dominant) and the second (subaltern) role in terms of coexistence and tactical positioning of the local, national, and transnational global economic actors and the local and national political and security factors in shaping political geography and geopolitics of countries in an age of globalization. This approach is strongly supported by the book to understand the emergence and the shift in post-Cold War geopolitics of the globalization in the Americas.

inevitable in a borderless world for liberal transnational economic actors, the cons build global social movements and social forum in many parts of the world (examples: Davos, Puerto Allegre) to block or curb the seamy side of economic liberalization and integration. As a matter of fact, instead of being the cons of globalization, those who are opposed to it prefer the appellation of "*Alter-Globalists*" as they try to present a popular and democratic alternative to poverty, precariousness, inequality, etc., generated by big firms and big corporations of economic globalization for many people in different parts of the world.

In this view, the sociopolitical and cultural claims of many local-global activists and, to some degree, academic works are focused on "*re-territorialization*" border-crossing practices and space border as transnational and global economic actors shrink the notion of national sovereignty and lift up barriers at national borders to free and speed up diverse flows and networks at local, national, regional, and global geographical scales.

## The Inter-American Space of Migrants' Networks and Network Cities

Analyzing transnational migrations linked to free trade between neighboring inter-American countries (Portes and Grosfoguel 1994, Zéphirin 2018) and as an aspect of geopolitics of globalization in the Americas refers largely in a theoretical standpoint to some economic and political accounts.

First, migrations are associated with origin and host countries in a migrant network (Massey 1987). Migrations use more than one actor and various geographical scales (Krissman 2005, Zéphirin 2005) before reaching their final targeted destination. Migration will continue to flow between high-income countries and mid- and low-income ones within the economic integrative bodies and their free-trade zones, until the economic and wage gap between the sending migrants' workers countries are narrowed or closed (Martin 2001).

Second, in a political point of view, the anti-immigrant sentiment seen in some high-income countries toward immigrants is that many citizens in countries hosting migrants enjoy low-paid jobs for foreign workers but refuse to repay to some degree some social benefits to migrants (Zéphirin 2017b). The opposition to migrants fuels political discourses and falls apart with political parties and national political systems.

Also, some anti-immigrant discourses aim at calming down political anger in societies than efficient immigration policy (Miller 1994, Czaika and de Haas 2013).

Additionally, immigration can be instrumented in both domestic politics and policy and international relations for war among powerful and powerless states (Weiner 1995, Mitchell 1982).

As a matter of fact, migration becomes a transnational issue within the economic regionalization-globalization raising and managing cross-border people movements as "compact" within the global governance framework to avoid human right abuses and discrimination of migrants. Thus, despite the "UN compact" over refugees and migrants presents some controversies to some researchers (Jorgen Carling 2020) who question the problematical reliability of the UN categorization of "refugees and immigrants."

This is an important step to take by applying the "UN migration compact" to manage the migration fear in domestic politics and policy toward migrants in an age of global migration crisis (Zolberg 2001, Castle and Miller 2018) and globalization (Sassen 1991).

Furthermore, studying migration and network cities as a matter of geopolitics of globalization in a theoretical standpoint refers to the connection of both immigration policy and migrant policy (Weiner 1995).

While immigration policy at the beginning is considered as consequential to geopolitics (economic, political, and security drivers on spaces and interstate relations), migrant policy in the mid or long term in both host and sending countries sparks geopolitics too in terms of spatially distributed or redistributed population in urban or rural areas, spatial and electoral redistricting in urban structures, and ethno-social and political mobilization in urban politics for inclusive policy.

All these elements in their interconnected causes and effects draw not only political demography and urban governance (Zéphirin 2020), but also political geography and geopolitics. The spatial repartition and human settlement patterns (Zephirin and Piantoni 2009) of migrants in the Caribbean, Central America, and South America in some major cities in the United States East Coast (examples are New York and Miami, Florida, among others) reveal a double geopolitics impact (local, national, and international).

On the one hand, the Caribbean, Central American, and South American migrant settlements mainly take place differently in the boroughs of New York (Zéphirin 2022). Example, while the Haitians and the Jamaicans are largely grouped in the county of Kings, the Dominicans, in majority, dwell in the Bronx and Queens (Portes and Grosfoguel 1994).

In the state of Florida, for example, the Cubans largely settle in Little Havana and downtown Miami.

The Haitians, in the beginning of their migration stream in Florida at the end of 1970, to a large extent established themselves in Little Haiti (which is actually heavily impacted by urban gentrification and urban relocation).

However, the urban areas of Broward and Boca Raton appear to be more mixed ethnic urban segments with people with higher socio-economic conditions and different origin and ethnocultural backgrounds. This type of spatial settlements and human interactions on space, politics, and power shapes, in one way or the other, the urban neighborhood artifacts and landscapes. As a result, migrants or the US citizens with Caribbean descent, by contributing to the structuration and restructuration of local urban territories, become a factor of political geography and geopolitics.

This is the geopolitics we see on space, politics, and power at local and national levels going over the local states of New York and Florida to extend itself to neighboring Caribbean countries of many US citizens (with Caribbean decent), through both national US senatorial or presidential elections and the United States's foreign policy toward some Caribbean countries. Obviously, it appears a triple local, national, and international dimension of geopolitics in migrants' populated urban areas.

In other words, migrations in cities are problematically connected to the geopolitics of globalization. This problematic articulation raises some theoretical explanations.

First, analyzing migration in network cities as geopolitics of globalization refers to the David Harvey (1985, 2001a, 2001b) theory of "network power" and "capitalist territorial expansion," Sassen Saskia's (1991) account of "global city," Gabriel Dupuis's (1997) theory of "network city," and "city government and urban governance" by Legales (1997).

The expansion of capitalism through globalization creates a "network power," allowing a type of geopolitics to enfold (Harvey, 1985, 2006) in decentralized "centers of commands" (Sassen 1991) of the globalized finance, investment, services, technology, goods, and humans in major global cities (Sassen 1991) managing the world political economy (Gilpin 1987) and the world political order.

The major world cities (Norton 2007) in major world regions (Pulsipher et al. 2015) and global cities (Sassen 1991) distribute the attributes of capitalism in the world system (Arrighi 1991, 1996) of the post-Cold War. In this view, human activities cross local, national, regional, and global geographical scales[61] (Sassen 2007, 11).

---

[61] Also, Sassen (2007, 11) has identified "four types of territoriality assembled out of the 'national' and 'global' elements... These four types of instances unsettle national state territoriality [...]. The territory of *the national is a critical dimension in play in all four.*"

> A first type of territoriality can be found in the development of new jurisdictional geographies... A second type of specialized assemblage that is contributing to a novel type of territoriality is the work of national state across the globe to construct a standardized global space for the operations of firms and markets... A third type of specialized assemblage can be detected in the formation of a global network of financial centers... A fourth type of assemblage can be found in the global networks of local

Cities within the globalization allow the diverse global flows to be integrated and form a "network." The "network cities" urban theory (Dupuis 1997, Taylor 2004, Castells 1996) appears to be reliable to conceptualize interactively the diverse global flows of humans, goods, trade, capital, information, and technology of globalization (as a mega geographical concept). The "network cities" theory within the globalization transcends all the basic and fundamental human geographical concepts of space, place, location, and region (Norton 2007; Sassen 2007, 12, 13, 14, 15).

In other words, Harvey's (2001a) theory of "network power," "capitalist territorial expansion," and "capitalist logic" of geopolitics

> activists and, more generally, in the concrete and often place-specific social infrastructure of global civil society. Global civil society is enabled by global digital networks and the associated imaginaries... While the third and the fourth types of territoriality might seem similar, they are actually not... Although these four types of emergent assemblages that function as territorialities are diverse, they all share certain features.
>
> First, they are not exclusively national or global but are assemblages of elements of each. Second, in this assembling they bring together what are often different spatio-temporal orders, [these are], different velocities and different scopes. Third, this can produce an eventful engagement, including contestations and what we might think of as a "frontier zone" effect a space that makes possible kinds of engagements for which there are no clear rules... Fourth, novel types of actors, initially often informal, political, or economic actors can emerge in the processes through which these assemblages are constituted. These novel actors tend to be able to access cross-border domains once exclusive to older established actors, notably national states. Finally, in the juxtaposition of the different temporal orders that come together in these novel territorialities, an existing capability can get redeployed to a domain with a different organizing logic. These emergent assemblages begin to unbundle the traditional territoriality of the national historically constructed overwhelmingly as a national unitary spatio-temporal domain. (Sassen: 2007, 13, 14, 15, 16, 17)

and an economic globalization is expressed as a matter of "network cities" theory, coupled with scattered actors on different geographical scales, territorial hierarchy, and urban structures. Analyzing the spatial consequences of globalization in terms of deterritorialization and reorganization of nation states, Sassen Saskia (2007) underlines the quasi takeover of national state institutions by big corporations as a matter of "deassemblage-reassemblage," impacting policy making and geographical scales[62] (Sassen 2007, 11) within a sovereign country.

Then the "global city" theory (Sassen 1991) connects the major world regions and world cities as a system encompassing the "center-periphery" or "centers-peripheries" relations in the world system and federating the different networks of the globalized economy.

---

[62]

> Where in the past most territories were subject to multiple systems of rules, the national sovereign gains exclusive authority over a given territory and at the same time this territory is constructed as coterminous with that authority in principle ensuring a similar dynamics in other nation-states. This in turn gives the sovereign the possibility of functioning as the exclusive grantor of rights. Territory is perhaps the most critical capability for the formation of the nation-state, while today we see ascend a variety of assemblages for which it is not, thus for the global regulators authority is more critical than territory... Globalization can be seen as destabilizing this particular scalar assemblage. What scholars have noticed is the fact the nation-state has lost some of its exclusive territorial authority to new global institutions. What they have failed to examine in depth is the specific, often the specialized arrangements inside the highly formalized and institutionalized national state apparatus aimed at instituting the authority of global institutions. This shift that is not simply a question of policy-making—it is about making a novel type of institutional space inside the state... critical components of the global are structure inside the national producing what I refer to as a spatial, and often highly specialized, denationalizing of what historically was constructed as national. (Sassen 2007, 11)

The political demography challenges problematically framed as an issue of urban governance put forth other dimensions of political geography and geopolitics (Weiner and Teitelbaum 2001, Mercille 2008, Zéphirin and Piantoni 2009, Zéphirin 2020). The great ethno-sociocultural diversity of the population in cities in the Americas in the context of economic regionalization-globalization shows up a significance of interest groups in practicing and taking advantages of the "global city" or of human mobility in "network cities" as an attempt to be part of "network power" associated with the "capitalist expansion logic" on neighboring regionalized spaces and countries (Sassen 1991, Dupuis 1997, Harvey 1985).

The difference in views of interest groups, perceptions, representations, and practices of the urban spaces in the context of globalization and its different approaches (Norton 2007) calls to review the theoretical obsolescence (in part or in whole) of the city government in urbanism (Choais 1991, Legales 1997) to the benefit of a more progressive theoretical account of urban governance for more participation and more ethno-social cultural fairness and inclusion in city planning and urban policy (Legales 1997, Zéphirin and Piantoni 2009).

Definitely, migration in network cities is an important subject in studying the geopolitics of globalization in the Americas and getting rid of the migration fear in political discourses.

## Theoretical Implications of Geoeconomics for the Research Community at Large

The conclusion blends some theoretical accounts, such as critical geopolitics and radical geopolitics (among others) involved in the interplay of geopolitics and geoeconomics in the inter-American globalization.

Radical geopolitics focuses on the key role-played by geoeconomic factors, outclassing geopolitical drivers (Mercille 2008). Radical geopolitics analyzes the interplay of geopolitics and geoeconomics in structuring foreign policy and, to some degree, domestic policies of capitalist states (Harvey 1985). As a matter of fact, radical geopolitics points out the preeminence (to a large extent) of transnational economic forces, big firms, and big corporations to the detriment of more traditional political actors.

However, while radical geopolitics and critical geopolitics share a lot of common problematic grounds, there are some differences between them in addressing the geopolitics as a matter of globalization in the Americas. It is important to underline them.

According to Mercille (2008),

> Critical geopolitics often neglects to investigate the political economic dynamics of policy, usually directing its attention to the analysis of discourses and representations as noted early on by Dodds and Sidaway (1994). True, it often includes political economy, but when it does, it either mostly discusses the institutional affiliation of elite groups but stops short of examining the workings of the political economic system which shapes policy-making or does not put enough emphasis on the (geo) economic factors behind policy... The political economic theoretical framework however is mostly concerned with interest groups and their motivations and downplays the significance of geoeconomic factors in shaping policy. (Mercille 2008, 572)

Also, the political economy theory stood out by Robert Gilpin (1987), while focusing on the interplay between international law, international economic and political analysis, to understand the world political and economic order pays attention to the "linkages between economics and politics in American foreign policy, rise and decline of hegemonic powers, challenge to the liberal economic order" (Malawer 1988, 308).

Additionally, it is important to note that social constructivism[63] and deconstructivism[64] plays an important role in problematizing the geopolitics of globalization by analyzing the interplay of discourse and power on the one hand through the dominant liberal economic regionalization policy, while forgetting migrants' living conditions, immigrants' rights, and official anti-immigrant discourse and the questioning of the triumphant ideology of market liberalization and integration as the end of history in the contemporary geopolitical configuration of major world regions while neglecting issues of global structural poverty and inequality, urban homelessness, exclusion, xenophobia, etc. (Fukuyama 1992; Derida 1994, 1998; Deacon 2006; Lebedeva and Lopez 2014; Vazquez-Arroyo 2019).

Furthermore, the construction of the Americas as a region, and its regionalization as a matter of political geography and geopolitics within the globalization, refers to some key theoretical accounts such as the "world-systems analysis theory" focusing on the international exchange and the use of natural resources of major world regions by countries identified as core, semiperiphery, periphery, and external regions in a logical of hierarchy of dependence within the contemporary capitalist regionalized-globalized economy (Wallerstein 2004, Cosma 2010).

Moreover, in order to understand the shift in the Americas' geopolitics as a means of economic regionalization-globalization, the theoretical accounts of critical geopolitics and political geography have been used to understand the "spatiality of social life and international relations," "space in critical social theory," "spatiality of power and contemporary capitalism," and "spatialization of international politics" (O'Tuathail 1996; Valdivieso 2012; Lefebvre 1974; Castells 1983; Soja 1989; Harvey 1985, 1989; Brenner et al. 2003). The role of powerful and hegemonic states' internal and external policy impacts on powerless states as a matter of framing geography as a means of power projection to pursue particular political, economic, and security agendas (Lacoste 1970, 1976). In this view, the shift in

---

[63] Michel Foucault
[64] Jacques Derida

geopolitics problematized as consequential to economic regionalization-globalization in the Americas, to a large extent, relates to the theoretical currents of "capitalist territorial expansion logic," "accumulation-dispossession," and "global cities as central command of the global economy" as in the process of shifting power among states and space in major world regions (Harvey 1985, 2006; Sassen 1991; Flint and Taylor 2018; Oslender 2016).

By the way, the end of the Cold War and the strategy of containment of communism in the Americas allowed democratic regimes to arise and replace autocratic and dictatorial ones (Stark and Jeffrey 1998). The democratic institutional process crossing the Americas during the 1990s went together with economic reforms, market liberalization, free trade, and economic integrations. This dynamic both segmented and integrated the Americas as a continent where diverse flows and networks are circulating. The integrated system of mobility of capital, labor, goods, and information on various geographical scales modified the concrete practices of territories by humans that become transnationalized.

The complexity in multipolar displacements (Zéphirin 2018) of people looking for better living conditions in integrative economic bodies composing the inter-American space (Smith 2001, Zéphirin 2016) in its causes and effects dismembers and reconstructs scales of territories across the Americas. The fact that some countries do better than others in creating more wealth and growth caused people located in peripheries and, in a lesser extent, those in semiperipheries to still dream to move to the wealthier northern part of the continent identified as the center of the globalization movement in the Americas (and the world). The discrepancy in salaries (and on migrants' remittances) from the south, the center, to the north of the Americas does not reduce the propensity to migrate, though it increases it (Martin 2001, Bogue 2012, Zéphirin 2016). Probably, the economic regionalization and subregionalization, while creating for many countries to build their material bases and their economic and infrastructural conditions to become "emerging economies," though the corollary salary gap did not stop yet transnational people movements.

While North America (mainly the US and Canada) champions the spread of economic integration message, allowing migrant workers and seasonal guest workers to cross borders and fill some low-paid and unskilled jobs and facilitating transnational investors to maximize their profits, however, national states are facing the pressure of overflow of labor migrants. Semiperiphery countries in the Americas are not strong enough economically to absorb the amount of job seekers coming from the peripheral ones while the well-off center of the economic globalization tightens the northern borders (United States) to unwanted labor migrants from South and Central Americas, organizing in a transnational caravan.

During the past decades, the Caribbean community has continued to grow in New York City, Jersey City, and Miami. The spatial distribution of the Caribbean immigrant population follows some socioeconomic, ethno-sociocultural, and sociopolitical networks and patterns in New York (and its five boroughs), for example. These factors, which drive spatial distribution and local political participation, are not in isolation from the whole multicultural urban society, urban economy, urban politics, and urban policy dynamics in New York, New Jersey, or Miami in the East Coast of the United States.

Consequently, in its diverse causes and effects, the Caribbean immigrants' urban location/relocation patterns reflect to some degree the US immigration policy and migrant policy in New York State, for example. The Caribbean immigrants' spatial distribution drives local political participation and, to some extent, political geographies.

Immigration remains a bone of contention among the states[65] (Miller 1994, 107) in the Americas. While the states agree on the principle of market liberalization, to some extent, they often show some disagreements on immigration[66] (Sassen 1996, 67). The fail-

---

[65] "From this perspective, problems of regulation commonly include a transparency gap between official and unofficial policies. Official policies, almost always considered restrictionist, are typically found to be symbolic rather than effective, repressive."

[66]

The existence of two different regimes for the circulation
of capital and the circulation of immigrants, as well as two

ure in managing the entirety of human flows following key capital centers of globalization reflects, at some point, some limitations of the complex interdependence approach in international relations[67] (Zurn 2013, 408, 409) to fully harmonize political tension consequential to market liberalization within main integrative economic bodies in the Americas. This is one of the practical and empirical factors showing new geopolitical parameters associated with transna-

---

equally different regimes for the protection of human rights and the protection of state sovereignty, poses problems that cannot be solved by the old rules of the game... Besides signalling a de facto transnationalizing of migration policy making, this also indicates the need to deconstruct 'the state' in its role in the migration process... Immigration can be seen as a strategic research site for the examination of the relation the distance, the tension between the idea of sovereignty as control over who enters and the constraints states encounter in making actual policy on this matter.

[67]

Global governance points to those sets of regulation which address denationalized problems, that are, problems which reach beyond national borders. The concept of global governance has two important implications. To begin with, by distinguishing governance structure from contents and actors, it becomes obvious that governance beyond the nation-state is possible, although a central authority or a 'world state' equipped with legitimate monopoly of the use of force is currently lacking (Roseneau 1992). Moreover, by requiring a common good-oriented justification of norms and rules, the concept of global governance also refers to a certain quality of international regulation... Accordingly, international cooperation includes more than just simple coordination between states to achieve a modus vivendi of interaction. (Zurn 2013, 408, 409)

Since the emergence of interdependence, research in international politics can no longer be reduced to the study of security and the military issues, of peace and war. World politics today is much more than that. Moreover, interdependence research brought non-state actors and, above all, international institutions to the fore. (Zurn 2013, 408)

tional migrations[68] (Smith 2001, 122; Mitchell 1992, 1998; Portes and Grosfoguel 1994; Portes and Rumbaut 1996; Forsythe, Baker, and Leonard 2001).

The raising and the mounting concerns of countries benefiting from migrant workforce in the periphery and the semiperiphery of globalization in the Americas (Goldin 2001) appear in many countries. Border security and security policy approaches sometimes go apart with some states' principles and values in terms of human rights and rule of law.

Within the globalization-regionalization of economies in the Americas, migration and diverse forms of mobility become an object of transnational issues, national security, and regional governance concerns[69] (Zurn 2013, 405, 408) that the geopolitical context did

---

[68]

I describe the inter-American migration system as a "loosely hinged" system. This conceptualization of "system" owes less to the architectural metaphors of Parson's structural-functionalism than it does to the physics metaphors of wolf's "open system," whose shape emerges from the contingent interplay of various levels and kinds of forces... I argue that the inter-American migration system encompassing Mexico, Central America, and the Caribbean emerged over time through the interaction of (1) government policies creating the conditions favoring migration, including those focused on economic development, immigration control regulation, and foreign policy; (2) changes in local, national, and global economies and population trends creating incentives to migrate; and (3) the internal logic by which migration becomes a semiautonomous process once it has become established through immigrant social networks. Such a framework offers advantages over the classic but more static framework identifying forces that "push" and "pull" migrants, by enabling us to analyze how these forces affect each other and evolve, currently and historically.

[69]

The current globalization literature is remarkably tacit on the issue of international peace and security...

not anticipate. The geopolitical aspect reflects the economic integration of the Western Hemisphere. The complex environment of the post-Cold War economic liberalization as a factor of geopolitics produces unseen or unwanted problems that, in their various causes and effects, become themselves the new contours of geopolitics of globalization in the Americas and their network cities. Managing flows of goods, people, and capital in network cities with diverse strategies of settlement, resettlement is in itself a factor of territorial formation, construction, and deconstruction revealing a geo-sociology and political geographies.

Return migrations and their remittances' practices and strategies question the role of migrants' money in local and regional territorial development connected to global flows and networks. While main global cities in the Americas, particularly in the northern high-income countries and cities as "command centers of the globalization" (Sassen 1991) interact with some middle-income South American countries and cities (such as Sao Paulo, Buenos Aires, Santiago in Chile) in the semiperiphery in exchanging important integrated

> By emphasizing the pressures that globalization puts on authoritarian states to foster liberalization, however, some writers more implicitly than explicitly have also connected globalization with the third peace strategy identified by Czempiel (1986) the "democratization of authoritarian societies" (peace through democracy, see especially the literature on diffusion of western norms, e.g.) (Sommons et al. 2006; Zurn 2013, 405)

> Globalization is not only said to be curbing the authority of nation-states and enforcing a convergence of national policies, but also disabling democracy and with it, the legitimacy of national political systems, altering the nature of sovereignty and thus ultimately transforming the fundamental structures of international politics from an anarchic to a global governance system... Global governance refers to the entirety of regulations put forward with reference to solving specific denationalization problems or providing transnational common goods. (Zurn 2013, 408)

influxes of capital, goods, human, and information, other cities and rural territories in low-income countries in the Americas' periphery are also impacted by the global flows in different ways, even to a lesser extent.

In this view, return migrants, largely from high-income countries and major North American global cities, transfer money and build houses, often based on archetypes from northern American megacities or global city centers and their suburbs.

Rural areas in the Americas' periphery are facing a mounting urban pressure (penetration of urbanization) in terms of the spread of new hybrid archetypes or, to a lesser extent, the importation of global model artifacts. In other words, people transnational movements in the Americas' network cities in the context of economic regionalization-globalization go over the formal link between global cities of the center and mega cities in the semiperiphery to reach the periphery and its urban-rural socio-spatial structures. Urban-rural territories in the Americas' periphery are transnationalized against themselves, through emigration, immigration, migrants, and return, migration processes on many interconnected neighboring loci. As a result, the network cities sparked by globalization and regional economic integration and their flows and networks encompass local, regional, national, and global cities. More importantly, the human settlement strategies and patterns of immigrants or dual citizens in mega or global cities often are legitimized by a personal project to return (home) to a particular "locality" in the Americas, but with a global or mixed sociocultural background.

All these elements are part of the new equation of migration in network cities and transnational territories in the Americas as geopolitics of globalization. Consequently, there is a need to revisit some theoretical approaches in local-regional development, the formation or the transformation process of region, the sociopolitical and spatial management of cultural and identity problems of "localities" facing global flows, mainstreaming migration development to promote local-regional development, and bridge endogenous local communities' development practices to global flows' attractiveness in order to revitalize endogenous local-regional potentials as a means of multiscale migration governance, political geographies, and geopolitics of globalization in the Americas.

As a matter of fact, the dominance of liberal transnational economic rationales in many parts of the world lays the problematic elements on the ground for the emergence of the concept of "geo-economics," outclassing traditional geopolitics. This shift in words changes the balance of power toward global economic actors to the detriment of territorialized political actors.

In an epistemological standpoint, social sciences disciplines and humanities tackled differently the theoretico-conceptual evolution and practices of globalization in the worldwide research community. Generally speaking, many pro-globalization economists and free-market advocates point out the need for pushing free trade, privatization, transnational accumulation, expansion, dispossession, and investment capital.

Geographers (social geographers and sociologists) study the diverse causes and effects of globalization in terms of "denaturalized dispossession," "uneven global integration," "inequality in power structures governing the globalization," the "map of the different networks and flows," "space-time compression and deterritorialization," "spatial fix and reterritorialization," "transfrontier space and transnationalism" (Harvey 2001a, 2006; Sparke 2014), "global cities," and "global migration" (Weiner 1995, Zolberg and Benda 2001, Sassen 1991).

Philosophers focus on deconstructing the triumphant borderless neoliberal discourse in trying to emphasize on global inequality and human rights. Political discourse supporting globalization underlines the key process of globalization as the sole alternative to economic prosperity, peace, security, and development. Thus, activists and globalists move their political and ideological speeches from an anticapitalist, anti-neoliberal, and an antiglobalist speech to a more pro-globalization to fix its seamy side in terms of poverty, inequality, human rights, and environmental threat as a matter of promoting worldwide and the alter-globalization movements.

Sociologists open their research field to study global sociology, global network society, social structures linked to transnational social classes, and global social movements. In this view, sociologists and cultural anthropologists collaborate on issues of ethnocultural change and adaptation in new globalized societies.

Sociologists (and social geographers) are interested in, among other things, poverty, inequality, homelessness, crime, socio-spatial structures, urban mobility, social movements, and solidarity at the global level, etc.

Historians show problematic interests to global transformation of political institutions, social and economic systems, globalization of institutions, and the evolution of social formation through time.

Also, historians find that elements of pre-globalization can be traced back to the European colonialist era. However, the globalization that the world is currently experiencing can be dated to the end of the 1980s and the beginning of the 1990s. Finally, critical scholars in social sciences who work on globalization are interested to highlight "winners and losers," functionality and dysfunctionality, and supporters and opponents to it.

Demographers are involved in studying demographic shifts, population composition, and demographic dynamics in the context of flows of global people movements across borders.

Economists dive into issues such as comparative advantage, employment opportunities, capital mobility and investments, wage attraction, and international labor migration, etc.

Lawyers are involved in regulation of space, border, free-trade zones, and deterritorialization of capital investments on the one hand, and gender inequality, poverty, human rights, etc., on the other hand.

Political scientists and international relationists focus on, among other things, transnational migrations' impact on political systems and governance, border crossing and border crossers' practices, and their consequences on international relations, national security, and human behavior.

Also, political scientists and international relations specialists who focus on global governance, debt cancellation, and poverty reduction are interested in harmonizing bilateral and multilateral politics and policy across the globe.

Geography, sociology, demography and cultural anthropology are some areas of the social sciences, and other academic disciplines (such as urbanism and architecture among others) dealing with urban planning, housing design and archetypes, urban-rural landscape formation, territoriality, urban geopolitics, territorial development, and governance in the general context of global economic competitivity rationales and local identity claims and protection.

Definitely, while the different branches of social sciences deal specifically with the problems generated by globalization, the interaction and the interconnectedness of the diverse causes and effects of the global liberal geoeconomics require scholars and researchers to explore a multidisciplinary approach to cover cutting-edge issues. In other words, the complexity of studying globalization as a new type of geopolitics calls for a multidisciplinary research approach in the research community at large.

Consequently, the significance of shifting drivers in geopolitics in a regionalized and globalized Americas is huge and impacts international migration networks in network cities. Labor migration is seen as a corollary of global economic liberalization and integration. The factor of migrant workers is an essential theoretical assumption of a migrant network (Massey 1987, Krissman 2005) and, to some extent, labor migrants from periphery countries to global cities in the global economy (Sassen 1991).

However, if labor migrants and migrant networks at the beginning (and on the short term) are dependent on economic liberalization and globalization in global cities and go together with a certain type of international politics, then the US global "structural power"[70]

---

[70] According to the

> structural power perspective on power shift…power stops where structure begins… Structural power emphasizes on] the importance of assigning responsibility to an agent for an exercise of power. (Lukes 2005)

> The social order and structures within which actors operate as powerful in and of themselves. (Forst 2017)

Structural power is to place primary emphasis on structures rather than agents in determining outcomes is clear and intuitive. (Joseph 2011)

Structural power is prior to questions of relational power. As Strange notes, the relative power of each party in a relationship is more, or less, if one party is also determining the surrounding structure of the relationship. (Strange 2015, 27; Kitchen and Cox 2019, 8)

The roots of structural power lie in relational advantage and system-making moments. When the rules, institutions, and norms of international order are up for contestation, relational power in that moment is crucial in establishing the structures from which structural power may subsequently flow. Such moments are infrequent; opportunities to establish structural power do not come along often. (Kitchen and Cox 2019, 8)

This point towards the idea that structural power might be as much unintentionally experienced as intentionally created, not established by force of will, but rather a direct consequence of a particular states' position in a particular domain that confers upon it particular advantages. (Kitchen and Cox 2019, 9)

Indeed, global finance and production are perhaps the most significant areas where structural power shapes the conditions under which other states must operate to the advantage of the United States. (Kitchen and Cox 2019, 10)

The conceptual use of "structural power" to analyze the shift in power from the traditional forms of the US power underlines some new forms of maintaining its hegemony.

"In short, the development of a regional economy conducive to the pursuit of US economic interests entailed the commitment of US military forces, and the reliance on US military preponderance to induce cooperation on American terms" (Stokes and Waterman 2017, 1047).

However, it is important to underline that this approach of "structural power" (Strange 2015) portraying the international order in the age of globalization faces some critics coming from preeminent scholars in the international relations

(Stokes and Waterman 2017, Kitchen and Cox 2019) and geopolitics on the long term downplayed the dependency to some degree, where migrant workers and international migrant network processes, become interconnected one to another on transnationalized network geographical loci (Zéphirin 2016, 2017, 2018).

As a result, the old restrictive geopolitical approach, its interstate relation policy, and its global economic liberalization rationales give way little by little to new politics of scale, political geographies, and geopolitics engendered by the self-produced interconnected migrant network, an international migration network, and reversible migration processes, crossing national borders of integrative economic bodies in their combined diverse causes and effects.

In other words, all these are new parameters and problematic elements to rethink the geopolitics[71] of globalization through migra-

---

field. In this view, Kitchen and Cox (2019, 6), citing Keohane (2000) and Palan (1999), write that "Strange's theory of structural power is underspecified and lacks precision…, and it is certainly true that the modalities of interaction between the four structures [production, finance, security and knowledge] is underdeveloped in Strange's work."

[71]

> Geopolitics [as contestation] is a continual process of defining the meaning of places, regions and territories in a politics of inclusion and exclusion (who does and does not "belong"). In other words, geography is always political and in some instances the politics is violent. (Flint and Taylor 2011, 33)

> While space, place, region, and (to some extent) scale can be seen as territorial, networks are seen as means to transcend territory. Networks are collections of nodes that are linked together. The nodes could be many things: terrorist cells, political activists, or businesses, for example. The nodes in a network can vary in their attributes what they are and what they do, [...]. Nodes are also distinguished by their centrality in the network, whether they are at the center of the network and linked to many other nodes or are they on the margins of the network and connected minimally. Some nodes are not even connected at all... Linkages can also take many different forms such as

tion in network cities and urban geopolitics[72] in the Americas (Flint and Taylor 2011, 54; Rokem and Freganese 2017, 6, 9; Paasche and Sidaway 2017; Sark 1986; Sidaway 2009).

The abovementioned theoretical accounts strongly impact and structure the problematization, methodological construction, and the analysis of the geopolitics of globalization and its diverse causes and effects regarding migration in network cities in the Western Hemisphere.

The theoretical tools allow to understand the transformation of the traditional US foreign policy and geopolitics into a new type of geopolitics shaped by geo-economic logic within globalization. As a matter of fact, the push by the United States's foreign regional policy (Western Europe also, to a lesser extent) for elected democratic governments in the Western Hemisphere associated with a liberal and market liberalization economic agenda marks a new development in

---

[72]

flows of migrants between cities… Linkages are of different strengths. (Flint and Taylor 2011, 54)

Ordinary urban geopolitics focuses among others on reconstructed and divided urban territory, producing patterns of contested socio-spatial formations, and creating new local geopolitical territories and zones of the urban outcasts. (Wacquant 2008)

Urban geopolitics is an open-ended framework covering processes of segregation and mobility across…cities. Through this lens, cities can be studied as both sites of divisions…places of opportunities for the emergence of new political arrangements, enabling the reconstruction of citizenship (Holston 2008) and fostering local ethnic minority integration… Bridging geopolitics into the mainstream of urban studies becomes critical in an era of growing neo-liberalization, ethno-nationalism, and international migration, where urban geopolitics can be a practical lens to encapsulate recent shifts in the contemporary urban present across a multitude of continents and geographical scales. (Rokem and Freganese 2017, 6, 9)

the US geopolitics in the Americas to allow capitalism and its market forces to control and extend its territories.

Now, the above answer to the central problematical hypothesis of the book transcending the empirical evaluation of economic liberalization and the theoretical framework to do research on global-regional flows and networks on transnational loci in the Americas raises the need to put the subject in perspective and explore other parameters in the problematic of geopolitics of globalization. Some particular themes emerge and appear to be of concern for policy makers, development practitioners, social reformers, human rights activists, researchers, scholars, etc. Among other things, regarding the geopolitics of globalization in the Americas, researchers and decision makers in a multidisciplinary approach should particularly pay attention to connect the dots between different fields and laterally problematize key issues, such as the use of natural resources by transnational corporations and big firms. As a matter of geopolitics, local ethnocultural claims for environmental protection and social and gender equality, transnational regional migration governance, international development cooperation, local development, local territorial governance, sociopolitical decentralized participation, migrants' remittances, capacity building, partnership development, sustainable development, foreign policy, regional security, and extra-hemispheric players with global intentions.

# References

Agnew, J. 1999. "Regions on the Mind Does not Equal Regions of the Mind." *Progress in Human Geography,* 23 (1): 91–96.

Agnew, J. 2003. *Geopolitics: Re-visioning World Politics* (2nd ed.). London: Routledge.

Agnew, J. and L. Muscara. 2012. *Making Political Geography* (2nd ed.). Lanham: Rowman and Littlefield Publishers Inc.

Arrighi, G. 1994. *The Long Twentieth Century.* London: Verso.

Barton, R. Jonathan. 2003. *A Political Geography of Latin America* (eBook). London: Taylor and Francis.

Bagnasco, A., and P. Le Gales. 2000. "Introduction: European Cities. Local Societies and Collective Actors?" In A. Bagnasco and P. Le Gales, eds. *Cities in Contemporary Europe.* Cambridge: Cambridge University Press.

Bhargava, Vinay. 2006. "Introduction to Global Issues." In *Global Issues for Global Citizens. An Introduction to Key Development Challenges.* Edited by Vinay Bhargava: 1–28. Washington, DC: World Bank.

Bogue, Donald J. 2012. *The Economic Adjustment of Immigrants to Twelve Nations of Latin American and Comparison with United States.* Population Research Center and Center on Aging. Chicago: The University of Chicago.

Budd, L. 1998. "Territorial Competition and Globalization: Scylla and Charybdis of European Cities." *Urban Studies,* 35: 663–686.

Choais, Francoise. 2014. *Urbanisme, Utopies et Réalités.* Paris: Seuil.

Chuhan, P. 2006. "Poverty and Inequality." In V. Bhargava (Ed.), *Global Issues for Global Citizens:* 31–50. Washington, DC: The World Bank.

Czaika, M. and H. de Haas. 2013. "On the Effectiveness of Immigration Policies." *Population and Development Review, 39* (3): 487–508.

Castells, M. 1996. *The Rise of Network Society.* Oxford: Blackwell.

Castles, S. and M. J. Miller. 2009. *The Age of Migration: International Population Movements in the Modern World* (4th ed.). Basingstock: Palgrave MacMillan.

Cosma, Sorinel. 2010. "Immanuel Wallerstein's World-System Theory." *Sine Loco. Ovidius Universitaty Constanta, Facultaty of Economic Sciencies*: 221–224.

Dalby, Simon. 1998. Globalization or global apartheid? Boundaries and knowledge in postmodern times. *Geopolitics*, 3: 1, 132-150, DOI:10.1080/14650049808407611.

Dalby, Simon. 1999. Against globalization from above: critical geo-politics and the World Order Models Project. *Environment and Planning I): Society and Space*, volume 17, pages 181-200.

Deacon, Roger. 2006. "Michel Foucault on Education: A Preliminary Theoretical Overview." *South African Journal of Education* 26, no. 2: 177–187.

Derida, Jacques. 1994. *Specters of Marx: The State of the Debt, the Work of Morning and the New International.* Translated by Peggy Kamuf. New York: Routledge.

Derida, Jacques. 1998. *Of Grammatology. Transl. Gayatri Chakravorty Spivak.* Connected edition. Baltimore: The John Hopkins University Press.

Di Meo, Guy. 1998. *Géographie sociale et territoire.* Paris: Nathan Université.

Dodds, J. K. and J. Sidaway. 1994. "Locating Critical Geopolitics." *Environment and Planning D. Society and Space,* 12:51–524.

Dupuis, Gabriel. 1991. *L'urbanisme des réseaux. Théories et méthodes.* Paris: Armand Colin.

Flint, Colin and Peter Taylor. 2018. *Political Geography: World Geography, Nation-State and Locality,* 7th edition. Routledge.

Flint, C. and P. J. Taylor. 2011. *Political Geography: World-Economy, Nation-State, and Locality,* 6th edition. Harlow: Prentice-Hall.

Forst, R. 2017. *Normativity and Power.* Oxford University Press.

Forsythe, P. David, Garry Baker, and Michèle Leonard. 2001. "US Foreign Policy, Democracy and Migration": 243–270, in *Global Migrants, Global Refugees, Problems and Solutions,* Zolberg Aristide and Benda Peter, Ed. New York/London: Berghahn Books.

Fukuyama, Francis. 1992. *The End of History and the Last Man.* Hamondsworth: Penguin.

Funkhouser, E., F. Ramos, and KPMG. P. Marwick. 1993. "The Choice of Migration Destination: Dominican and Cuban Immigrants to the Mainland United States and Puerto Rico." *The International Migration Review (IMR)* 27, no. 3: 537–556.

Giddens, A. 1999. *Runaway World.* Cambridge: Polity Press.

Gilpin, Robert. 1987. *The Political Economy of International Relations.* Princeton, NJ: Princeton University Press.

Goldin, Ian. 2006. "Globalizing with Their Feet: The Opportunities and Costs of International Migration" in *Global Issues for Global Citizens* (ed. Vinay Bhargava): 105–121. Washington, DC: The World Bank Report.

Goldstone, J. A., E. F. Kaufmann, and M. D. Toft. 2012. *Political Demography: How Population Changes Are Reshaping International Security and National Politics.* Boulder and London: Paradigm Publishers.

Guntram, H. Herb. 2007. The Politics of Political Geography. In Cox, *Handbook of Political Geography.* P. 21-40. On Academia. [09:42 1/8/2007 4952-Cox-Ch01.tex] Paper Size: a4 paper. Job No: 4952 Cox: Handbook of Political Geography.

Guzzini, Stephano. 2005. "The Concept of Power: A Constructivist Analysis." *Millennium Journal of International Studies,* 33 (3): 495–521.

Hayot, A. and A. Sauvage (sous la Dir.). 2000. *Le projet urbain. Enjeux, expérimentations et professions.* Paris: Editions de la Villette.

Harvey, David. 1985. "The Geopolitics of Capitalism." In D. Gregory and D. Urry (eds.) *Social Relations and Spatial Structures*: 128–163. London: Macmillan.

Harvey, David. 2001a. "Globalization and the Spatial Fix." *Geographische Revue,* 2: 23–30.

Harvey, David. 2001b. *Spaces of Capital: Toward a Critical Geography.* New York: Routledge.

Harvey, David. 2003. *The New Imperialism.* Oxford: Oxford University Press.

Harvey, David. 2006. *Spaces of Global Capitalism. Towards a Theory of Uneven Geographical Development.* London: Verso.

Hillman, S. Richard and D'Agostino J. Thomas. 2003. *Understanding the Contemporary Caribbean*. Colorado: Lynne Reinner Publisher.

Huntington, Samuel. 1996. *The Clash of Civilization and the Remaking of World Order*. With a new foreword of Zbignew Brzezinski. New York: Simon and Shuster.

Joseph, J. 2011. "Structural Power". In K. Dowding, ed. *Encyclopedia of Power*. SAGE, PP. 637-640.

Kaltmeier, O, A. Tittor, D. Hawkings, and E. Rohland. 2020. *The Routledge Handbook to the Political Economy and Governance of the Americas*. London / New York: Routledge.

Kitchen, Nicholas and Michael, Cox. 2019. "Power, Structural Power, and American Decline." www.http//.reprints.lse.ac.uk.

Knight, W. Frank. 1990. *The Caribbean—The Genesis of a Fragmented Nationalism* (2nd ed.). New York, Oxford University Press.

Krissman, Fred. 2005. "Sin Coyote Ni Patron: Why the Migrant Network Fails to Explain International Migration." *International Migration Review (IMR)* 39, no.1 (Spring): 4–44.

Lebedeva, Alexandra and Mercedes-Maria, Lopez. 2014. *The Construction of Immigrants' Identity in the EU. A Foucauldian Discourse Analysis of EU Common Migratory Policy*. Umca University.

Lefebvre, H. 1977. *De l'Etat: le mode de production étatique* 3. Paris: Union Générale d'Editions.

Lefebvre, H. 1978. *De l'Etat: les contradictions de l'Etat moderne* 4. Paris: Union Générale d'Editions.

Lefebvre, H. 1991. *The Production of Space*. Oxford: Blackwell.

Le Gales, P. 1995. "Du gouvernement des villes à la gouvernance urbaine." *Revue française de science politique* 45, no. 1: 57–95.

Lukes, S. 2005. *Power: a radical view*. 2nd ed., Houndmills, Basingstoke, Hamshire, New York: Palgrave Macmillan.

Malawer, S. Stuart. 1988. "The Political Economy of International Relations by Robert Gilpin." In *Maryland Journal of International Law* 12, no. 2, article 6: 307–311.

Mamadouh, V. and M. Muller. 2017. "Political Geography and Geopolitics." In *European Regions and Boiundaries. A Conceptual*

*History.* Diana Mishkova and Balazs Trencsenyi: 259–279. New York: Berghahan.

Manigat, Leslie. 1991. *L'Amérique latine au XXième siècle: 1889–1929.* Paris: Seuil.

Mercille, Julien. 2008. "The Radical Geopolitics of US Foreign Policy Geopolitical and Geoeconomic Logic of Power." *Political Geography—Elsevier,* vol. 27: 570–586.

Martin, L. Philip and Edward J. Taylor. 2001. "Managing Migration: The Role of Economic Policies": 95–120. In Aristide Zolberg and Peter M. Benda, *Global Migrants Global Refugees. Problems and Solutions.* New York: Berghahn Books.

Massey, S. Douglas et al. 1987. *Return to Aztlan: The Social Process of International Migration from Western Mexico.* Berkeley: University of California.

Massey, S. Douglas. 1993. "Theories of International Migration," *Population and Development Review,* 19 (3): 431–466.

Merlin, P. 1991. *L'urbanisme,* Que sais-je? Paris: PUF.

Miller, J. Mark. 1994. "Introducing the Critical Transparency School of Immigration Analysis," in *Controlling Immigration. A Global Perspective*: 107–112. Wayne A. Cornelius, Philip L. Martin and James F. Hollifield, eds. Stanford, California: Stanford University Press.

Mitchell, Christopher. 1992. "Introduction: Immigration and US Foreign Policy Toward the Caribbean, Central America, and Mexico": 1–3. In Mitchell, Christopher. *Western Hemisphere Immigration and the United States Foreign Policy.* The Pennsylvania State University.

Mitchell, Christopher. 1989. "International Migration, International Relations and Foreign Policy." *International Migration Review (IMR)* 23, no. 3: 681–708.

Nolte, D. and E. L. Webner. 2015. *Routledge Handbook of Latin American Security.* London: Routledge.

Nolte, Detlef. 2013. "The Dragon in the Backyard: US Visions of China's Relations Toward Latin America." In *Relationes Internationales. Pap. Polit.* (Bogota-Colombia) 18, no. 2: 587–598.

Norton, William. 2007. *Human Geography* (6th ed.). New York: Oxford University Press.

O'Tuathail, Gearoid. 1996. *Critical Geopolitics. The Politics of Writing Global Space.* Minneapolis: University of Minnesota Press.

Oslender, Ulrich. 2016. *The Geography of Social Movements. Afro-Colombian Mobilization and the Aquatic Space.* Durham: Duke University Press.

Portes, Alejandro and G. Ruben Rumbaut. 1996. *Immigrant America.* Los Angeles: University of California Press.

Portes, A. and R. Grosfoguel. 1994. "Caribbean Diasporas: Migration and Ethnic Communities." *The Annals of the American Academy of Political and Social Science* 553: 48–69.

Scheman, L. R. 2003. *Greater America: A New Partnership for the Americas in the 21st Century.* New York: New York University Press.

Paasche, F. Till and James D. Sidaway. 2017. "The Urban and the Geopolitical as Categories of Theory and Practice: Front-Line Reflections." In *Interventions in Urban Geopolitics, Political Geography*: 1–9.

Rokem, J and S. Fregonese, A. Ramadan, E. A. Pascucci, G. Rosen, I. Charmey, T. F. Paasche, and J. D. Sidaway. http://dx.doi.org/10.1016/j.palgeo.2017.04.004.

Puntigliano, A. R. 2016. *21st Century Geopolitics: Integration and Development in the Age of Continental States—Territory, Politics and Governance* 5, no. 4: 478–494. Routledge, Taylor, Francis.

Pulsipher, Lydia Mihelic and Alex Pulsipher. 2015. *World Regional Geography Concepts* (3rd ed.), W. H. Freeman and Company. New York: Macmillan.

Rivas, Simon. 2020. *Geopolitics. Sine Loco.*

Roberts, Anthea and Nicolas, Lamp. 2021. *Six Faces of Globalization. - Who Wins, Who Loses, and What it Matters.* Cambridge (MA): Harvard University Press.

Rokem, Jonathan and Sara, Freganese. 2017. "Interventions in Urban Geopolitics." In *Interventions in Urban Geopolitics, Political Geography*: 1–9. Rokem, J and S. Fregonese, A. Ramadan, *E.*

*A.* Pascucci, G. Rosen, I. Charmey, T. F. Paasche, and J. D. Sidaway, http://dx.doi.org/10.1016/j.palgeo.2017.04.004.

Sassen, Saskia. 1996. *Losing Control? Sovereignty in an Age of Globalization. New York:* Columbia University Press.

Sassen, Saskia. 2007. "Deciphering the Global: Its Spaces, Scales and Subjects." *Social Thought and Research* 29: 3–18.

Sark, R. 1986. *Human Territoriality: In Theory and History.* Cambridge: Cambridge University Press.

Sidaway, D. James. 2009. "Shadows on the Path: Negotiating Geopolitics on an Urban Section of Britains' South-West Coast Path." *Environment and Planning D Society and Space* 27, no. 6: 1091–1116.

Silva, A. Micael. 2019. "American Crossings: Border Politics in the Western Hemisphere." *Contexto International* 41, no. 1 (Jan.–Apr.): 235.

Smith C. Robert. 2001. "Current Dilemmas and Future Prospects of the Inter-American Migration System," in A. R. Zolberg and P. M. Benda, eds. *Global Migrants Global Refugees. Problems and solutions*: 121–167. New York: Berghahn Books.

Soja, E. W. 1989. *Postmodern Geographies: The Reassertion of Space in Critical Social Theory.* London: Verso.

Sparke, M. 2002. "Not a State, but More Than a State of Mind: Cascading Cascadias and Geoeconomics of Cross-Border Regionalism." In M. Perkmann and N. Sum, eds. *Globalization, Regionalization, and Cross-Border Regions:* 212–240. London: Palgrave.

Sparke, M. 2014. *Defining Globalization: Work in Progress.* University of Washington (Found on Academia Online Research Engine). Draft entry on Globalization for *The International Encyclopedia of Geography: People, the Earth, Environment, and Technology,* edited by Douglas Richardson et al, forthcoming from Wiley.

Sparke, M. 2007. "Geopolitical Fears, Geoeconomic Hopes, and the Responsibilities of Geography." *Annals of the Association of American Geographers* 97, no. 2: 337–348.

Stark, Jeffrey. 1998. "Globalization and Democracy in Latin America." In *Fault Lines of Democracy in Post-Transition Latin*

*America*: 67–96. Edited by Felipe Aguero and Jeffrey Stark. Miami: North-South Center Press at the University of Miami.

Stokes, Doug and Kit, Waterman. 2017. "Security Leverage, Structural Power and US Strategy in East Asia." *International Affairs.* Vol. 93:1039–1060. *Oxford University Press—The Royal Institute of International Affairs.*

Strange, S. 2015. *States and Markets.* Bloomsbury Publishing.

Taylor, P. J. 2004. *World City Network: A Global Urban Analysis.* New York: Routledge Taylor and Francis Group.

Valdivieso, J. P. 2012. "Understanding Critical Geopolitics." *Sine Loco.*

Vazquez-Arroyo, Y. A. 2019. "The Political Import of Deconstruction. Derida's Limits?: A Forum on Jacques Derida's Specters of Marx After 25 Years, Part 1." *Contexto International* 41, no. 3 (Sept.–Dec.): 621–642.

Wacquant, L.2008. *Urban Outcasts—A Comparative Sociology of Advanced Marginality.* Cambridge: Polity Press.

Wacquant, L. 2016. Revisiting territories of relegation: Class, ethnicity and state in the making of advanced marginality, *Urban Studies,* 53(6): 1077–1088.

Wallerstein, I. 1984. *Politics of the World-Economy.* Cambridge: Cambridge University Press.

Wallerstein, Immanuel. 2004. *World-System Analysis. An Introduction.* Durham: Duke University Press.

Weiner, Myron. 1995. *The Global Migration Crisis—Challenge to States and to Human Rights.* New York: Harper Collins.

Zéphirin, Romanovski. 2005. *Le Champ migratoire haïtiano-guyanais: étude des causes et effets politiques, socio-économiques et spatiaux. Multipolarité et réversibilité dans le système migratoire interaméricain.* Aix-en-Provence: Thèse de Doctorat sous la direction de Hervé Domenach, Université Aix-Marseille III, Faculté de Droit, d'Economie et des Sciences-IUAR (Institut d'Urbanisme et d'Aménagement Régional).

Zéphirin, R. and F. Piantoni. 2009. "Les stratégies d'accès au logement des Haïtiens dans l'agglomération de Cayenne Comme facteurs de restructuration urbaine." Revue *L'Espace Politique* 6, no. 3: 1–12, Mai. En ligne, www.l'espacepolitique.revues.org

Zéphirin, Romanovski. 2016. *Les réseaux de migrants haïtiano-guyanais dans l'espace américain.* Paris: L'Harmattan (Collection Questions Contemporaines).

Zéphirin, Romanovski. 2017a. "The Politics and Policy Implications of Widespread Immigrations in French Guyana." In *Migrants: Public Attitudes, Challenges and Policy Implications*, edited by Stuart Rodriquez, 59–110. New York: NOVA Science Publishers. Collection Immigration in the 21st Century: Political, Social and Economic Issues.

Zéphirin, Romanovski. 2017b. "Why Migrant Network and International Migration Cannot Be Schematically Separated?" In *Migrants: Public Attitudes, Challenges and Policy Implications*, edited by Stuart Rodriquez, 275–283. New York: NOVA Science Publishers. Collection Immigration in the 21st Century: Political, Social and Economic Issues.

Zéphirin, Romanovski, 2018. "The Americas' Multi-Polar Displacements as a New Pattern in Haitian-French-Guyanese Migrations." *International Migration Journal*—IOM. Available Online (01 June), https://doi.org/10.1111/imig.12470.

Zéphirin, Romanovski. 2020. Political Demography and Urban Governance—Implications for Latin America and the Caribbean. London-Singapore: Palgrave Macmillan.

Zéphirin, Romanovski. 2022. The *Urban* Settlement of the Caribbean Immigrants in Brooklyn—New York as Politics and Policy Issues. *Journal of Public Policy and Administration*, vol. x, no. (x): x-x. doi: 10.11648/j.xxx.xxxxxxxx.xx (Forthcoming).

Zurn, M. 2013. "Globalization and Global Governance." In *Handbook of International Relations.* Carlsnaes, W. T. Risse, and A. B. Simmons. (Ed.). 401–423. London: SAGE.

# INDEX

# ABOUT THE AUTHOR

Romanovski Zéphirin, PhD, teaches human geography and world issues at the City University of New York (CUNY-BMCC), USA. He is an editorial board member of *Journal of Public Policy and Administration (JPPA)* at Science Publishing Group in New York, USA. He is also a peer reviewer for the academic journals of *Development in Practice*, Oxford, the UK, and *La Revue Européenne des Migrations Internationales (REMI)*, Poitiers, France.

His work focuses on economic regionalization, globalization, political geography, geopolitics, international relations, foreign policy, immigration, political demography, territorial development, cities, and the Americas.

He is a best-selling author at Palgrave Macmillan, and his best seller was featured on CNN, Forbes Inc., and BookAuthority, and ranked sixth among eleven best new demography books in the world in 2021.